I need a Job, Now What?!™

by Janet Garber

SILVER
LINING
BOOKS
NEW YORK

Copyright © 2001 by Silver Lining Books
ISBN 0760720665

For information contact:
Silver Lining Books
122 Fifth Avenue
New York, NY 10011

First Edition
This edition was published by Silver Lining Books.

Printed and Bound in the United States of America

Other titles in the Now What?!™ series:

I'm Turning on my PC, Now What?!
I'm Turning on my iMac, Now What?!
I'm in the Wine Store, Now What?!
I'm in the Kitchen, Now What?!
I Need to Get in Shape, Now What?!
I Haven't Saved a Dime, Now What?!

introduction

It was Neil's third job elimination in as many years.
"Is it me or my career choice or what?" he lamented. It was clear
he was smart and capable. But let's face it, every industry
goes through a period of retrenching. In Neil's case it
was the Internet industry. Just two years ago it was
the insurance business. Who knows which industry
will be hit next? The important thing is to be prepared for it. That's where **I need a Job, Now What?!**
comes in to save the day. It's filled with down-to-earth
help on the fine art of finding and keeping a job. Help
that comes firsthand from Janet Garber, author as well as
human resource professional. Learn the trade secrets of resumé
writing, interviewing, and landing a job—or starting your own
business.

Whether you are just starting out in your first job, returning to
work, or wondering how to bounce back from a layoff, this book is
for you. Chin up. The cavalry is just a few pages away.

Barb Chintz
Editorial Director, the *Now What ?!*™ series

table of contents

Starting 6

Knowing yourself **8** Gauging interests **10** Setting sights high **12** Exploring dreams **14** Sizing up skills **16** Assessing options **18** Responding to demand **20** Sharpening skills **22** Rating experience **24** Now what do I do? **26**

Resumés 28

Putting your life on paper **30** Parts of the whole **32** Organizing for effect **34** Tailoring your track record **36** Emphasizing strengths **38** A resumé without jobs **40** Electronic resumé **42** Writing cover letters **44** Customizing letters **46** Now what do I do? **48**

Job resources 50

Print ads **52** Online ads **54** Career services **56** Employment agencies **58** Headhunters **60** Research **62** Keeping on track **64** Now what do I do? **66**

Networking 68

Getting the word out **70** Professional meetings **72** Informational interviews **74** Finding a mentor **76** Cold calls **78** Now what do I do? **80**

Interviews 82

The process **84** In the waiting room **86** Trade secrets **88** The tangibles **90** Subjects to avoid **92** The intangibles **94** The tough questions **96** After the interview **98** Sample thank-you letters **100** A second interview **102** Now what do I do? **104**

Refining the search 106

A stalled search **108** Review your skills **110** Check your tactics **112**
Adjust your focus **114** Find support **116** Consider relocating **118**
Now what do I do? **120**

Job offers 122

Evaluating the job **124** Negotiating salary **126** Evaluating benefits **128**
Negotiating benefits **130** Accepting an offer **132** Updating your
network **134** Turning down an offer **136** Now what do I do? **138**

On the job 140

You did it, now what?! **142** Settling down **144** Fitting in **146**
Getting along **148** Staying out of trouble **150**
Getting ahead **152** Now what do I do? **154**

Be your own boss 156

Instead of a job **158** Do you really want to be
on your own? **160** Working at home **162**
Running a business outside your home **164**
Being a freelancer, e-lancer, contractor, or
consultant **166** Now what do I do? **168**

Index 170

Starting

Knowing yourself 8
Start with your strong points

Gauging interests 10
Analyze the way you like to work

Setting sights high 12
Build on what you do well

Exploring dreams 14
Find out how to make them real

Sizing up skills 16
Evaluate marketable expertise

Assessing options 18
Identify when and where you want to work

Responding to demand 20
Analyze what employers value

Sharpening skills 22
Pursue the right education and training

Rating experience 24
Determine how to use it to advantage

Now what do I do? 26
Answers to common problems

One of the most valuable personal characteristics in the job market
is the ability to work well with other people.

knowing yourself

Build your job search to take advantage of who you really are

your twentieth. This time, though, you are in charge. Yes. You are the boss of your job search. So let's talk about how you can begin your search in a way that ensures success.

Smart job hunting requires a bit of self-knowledge. Just as one key does not open every door, one person cannot do every job. Recognizing your strongest traits can help you find a good job fit. So make like a detective and grab a magnifying glass—prepare to examine yourself, inside and out.

Consider your personality, but try to do it without judging yourself positively or negatively. What stands out about you? For example:

■ If you are assertive, persuasive, articulate, good with people, but impatient with paperwork, bored with detail, and indifferent to computers, maybe sales is the right line of work for you.

■ If you are quiet and self-contained, like orderly workdays and precise tasks, something in the accounting field might suit you. Or if math is not your thing, you might find copyediting a snap.

■ If you enjoy working with people and organizing projects, you might make a good manager.

■ If you are adventurous, someone who thrives on pushing the envelope, living on the edge, and you feel alive only when pumped up with fight-or-flight adrenaline, an office job probably is not the thing for you. You might be better off as an entrepreneur or taking a job in an industry that rewards taking risks.

■ If you are a loner and like to work on your own, directing yourself, look at jobs that are solitary; research or writing could be the answer.

SK YOURSELF

I have no idea what type I am. Now what?

Think back to when you were a child. How did your relatives and teachers characterize your personality? What did you feel about their assessments? Your strengths lie somewhere in between what they observed then and what you perceived in yourself.

How important are people skills?

One of the most valuable personal characteristics in the job market is the ability to work well with other people. It entails more than thoughtfulness toward others; it also requires a self-respect and self-confidence on your part that allows your interest in others to be wholehearted.

Interpersonal skills not only help you to work more efficiently; they can also help you land a job. Although these skills seem to come naturally to some individuals, they can usually be acquired by anyone. Two starting points:

1. Concentrate on becoming a better listener.
2. Make a conscious effort to be more considerate of your colleagues' point of view.

If you just can't get the hang of it, some personal sessions with a private counselor or psychologist can help you develop these career-enhancing habits.

What if I like working with people well enough, but I also need time to myself?

You would probably prefer solitary challenges such as major number-crunching bouts in a quiet cubicle, or ferreting out exacting microscopic secrets in a lab, or tapping out articles or research reports at home. But your people skills will still come in handy in those conferences and planning meetings every business thrives on.

HOW LONG WILL MY JOB HUNT TAKE?

Lucky breaks sometimes occur, but a serious job search can take about six months. It may speed up if you know exactly what kind of job you want. It can fly by if you have good experience in a field in which there's a shortage of trained people.

gauging interests

Understand how you work best, then factor it into your job hunt

Personality and aptitude tests aren't infallible, but they can help you understand the nature of your character. Here's a quick one that can start you thinking about where your abilities lie. (A key to your answers is on the bottom of the next page.)

	Yes	No
1. Do you find yourself helping others more often than not?		
2. Do you live for the moment rather than planning ahead?		
3. Do you love working with abstract ideas?		
4. Do you learn best by ignoring instructions and trying things?		
5. Are you constantly coming up with new ideas?		
6. Do you like to take action and leave the reflecting to others?		
7. Do you often start projects and let others fill in the details?		
8. Do you work best alone?		
9. Do you enjoy explaining things to other people?		
10. Are you an individualist?		
11. Do you like getting approval from others?		
12. Do you take a methodical approach to problems?		
13. Do you like to try to size up people?		
14. Do you often worry when you see someone who is sad?		
15. Do you dislike routine tasks?		

ASK YOURSELF

What's your type?

Idealists like Gandhi favor teaching. Guardians like Colin Powell gravitate toward management. Artisans like Elvis prefer the arts and working with instruments. Rationals like Marie Curie enjoy science, systems and technology.

Who do you admire?

Think back to places where you have worked before, or when you were in school. Is there a boss, a fellow employee or a former teacher whose presence made a significant impression on you? List the things you like about the way that person did a job. Do you have some of the same tendencies?

KEY TO APTITUDE TEST

If you answer yes to these questions:	It indicates that you tend to be:	Consider careers in fields such as:
1, 9, 11, 14	A caregiver	social work or nursing
2, 6, 7	A doer	entrepreneurship, sales, police work
9, 13, 15	A motivator	psychology, writing, teaching, acting
3, 8, 12	A logician	science, engineering, law, parks management
4, 5, 10, 15	An artist	design, architecture, landscaping

If all your answers are not in one category, you may be more of a generalist. Consider jobs that require interests in several fields, such as film director, policy planner, or editor for illustrated books.

setting sights high

Nothing fires up a job search faster than the prospect of getting paid for doing something you love

Here's an easy question: When you were little, what did you want to be when you grew up? Now think about why you were attracted to such an activity, and whether the child in you still wants to do that. If so, maybe you can adapt the idea of it into a new job.

For instance, did you want to be a fireman? If you craved excitement then *and* now, maybe a job as an ER technician or a paramedic holds appeal. Did you want to be a teacher? Perhaps that desire to help means you'd be effective in a computer support or customer service position.

Don't let your grown-up reality deter you in this exercise. You can be your own worst enemy when you let your fears for the future overwhelm you and squelch all dreams and ambitions, or if you allow critical voices from the past to interrupt your ambitions.

Sure, it may be that your dreams are not so practical, or that you've outgrown them or they've morphed into something a little different. But it's worth the effort to plumb the depths to see what's lying at the ocean's bottom of your secret longings. You'll go further if you begin by acknowledging them.

# ASK YOURSELF

What activities, hobbies, and pastimes give you the greatest pleasure? What is it you enjoy the most about these things? Is there a clue here about what you could tie in to a career?

Is there any activity you do that puts you in a state of bliss, allows you to zone out and lose the sense of time passing? Do you look up and can't believe three hours have gone by? Could this be your passion in life? Can you turn it into your job?

How do you picture yourself in your dreams? Are you toiling alone or working with others? Is it in a quiet, calm environment or a busy, noisy, happening one? Are you concentrating on one project at a time or glorying in multitasking? What would you be doing in the best of all possible worlds?

Is there a way to get to that place from where you are now? What would you have to do, step by step, day by day, hour by hour? Realistically, is your hobby a potential job?

With your feet firmly planted on the ground, can you honestly say that your amateur status as a stargazer might change to a professional one if you went for the right training? Could it ever pay the mortgage? Or perhaps you can incorporate it into a related job, say, as a science teacher, a curator in a science museum, or a science textbook writer? Or could you work in a shop that makes lenses for telescopes?

exploring dreams

Identify the perfect job and go for it

How do you find out if you still have any dreams or ambitions? First, do some old-fashioned soul-searching. Or try consulting with a career counselor—a person who's trained to help you analyze your ideas and match them up to real-life possibilities. How do they do this? One way is by having you take tests for aptitudes and interests. Another way is to talk with you about your goals and how you developed them.

If a private career counselor is out of the question, consider a job-counseling workshop, available in most cities at various times of the year. Workshops are group sessions with one or more counselors who help you explore job possibilities that suit your aptitudes and interests. A workshop removes you from familiar surroundings for a day, a weekend, or even a week or two, so that you can sort out priorities and find a new outlook on your future.

Or join a job-search club to bounce ideas off a group of other job-seekers (and in the bargain get moral support to ease the frustrations that arise during job hunting). You can form your own with friends who might have been laid off, or look on the Internet for non-profit groups in your area, or ask career counselors to give you recommendations.

Putting your long-lost dreams and ambitions to work in a new job can do more to make your work satisfying—and eventually profitable—than any other factor. So don't think of this kind of exploration as a waste of time. Consider it an investment.

WHAT'S OUT THERE: JOB COUNSELING

1. *A Consumer's Guide to Retail Job-Hunting Services*, National Business Employment Weekly, 800-730-1111

2. *What Color is Your Parachute? 2000* by Richard Nelson Bolles, Ten Speed Press

3. The Five O'Clock Club at www.fiveoclockclub.com

4. Crystal-Barkley Corporation, 800-333-9003, or www.careerlife.com, offers books, courses, and coaching

5. "Career counseling" sections in the yellow pages, and Web sites for the same on the Internet

Job Growth by Industry

If possible match your dream job to a burgeoning industry. See the list below to see which industries are booming and which are lagging.

Industry	1992-2005 (Percentage change)
Health services	+43.4
Educational services	+28.4
Food services	+33
Social services	+93.1
Personnel supply services	+56.6
Computer services	+95.7
Hotels/lodging	+40.5
Amusement/recreation	+39.1
Management/public relations	+69.5
Child-care services	+73
Agricultural services	+40.5
Motion picture production	+60.8
Apparel manufacturing	-24.4
Telephone communications	-20.6
Electronics manufacturing	-16.3
Textile manufacturing	-15
Oil and gas extraction	-14.3
Steel manufacturing	-10.5
Mining	-6.8
Motor vehicle manufacturing	-6.1
Federal government	-5.2
Chemicals	-4.0
Food processing	-0.4

Source: U.S. Dept. of Labor Bureau of Labor Statistics

sizing up skills

You can trade on what you're good at

What are your current skills and abilities? When you were in school, you may have received high marks for certain courses. Bosses and coworkers from your past jobs may have praised you for certain skills and abilities in which you excel. These are all marketable traits—signposts to point you toward the job categories you're best suited for. They can be readily put to work and will help to ensure your future success. A good job fit, after all, is a marriage of your experience and your natural inclinations.

Even if you're currently employed, you need to keep on stretching your skills. Observe the best people in your field and in related fields. Consider exactly what they are able to do well, and try to cultivate those same skills, even if you don't find them necessary at the moment, let alone interesting. Should there be cutbacks in your industry, people who can do a number of different tasks will be more employable.

Marc G.
Strong math apptitude
Good group organizer
Detail oriented

Kelly M.
Major interest in chemistry
Excellent research abilities
Likes to work alone

Jason T.
Creative writing skills
School events coordinator
Sharp sense of humor

IF YOU CAN'T TURN ON A COMPUTER

Computers and Web sites now rule the marketplace. If you are afraid of them, get over it. Computer training is paramount for every worker, from those in entry-level positions to the most sophisticated execs.

If you already have computer skills, train yourself in new programs that are being introduced in your industry. Once you are working, your company is likely to pay for courses and the cost of new programs you need for the job. When you are not working, find out if your library, the local Y, community college, or continuing education program at your high school offers courses. You are always a more valuable employee at the head of the electronic pack.

If you have never learned how to use a computer, run to your nearest continuing education program (check the local high school or community college for one) and start with basic training. Otherwise, you are needlessly limiting your working future. There are few jobs that don't require a minimum knowledge of computers.

Computer quiz: Do you know this?

1. Can you format a letter or report?

2. Can you change the font?

3. Can you make revisions in a document?

4. Can you use a spell-check function?

5. Can you store a document and retrieve it?

If you can't perform these basic word-processing tasks, quit putting it off; you need to take at least a one-day computer course. Or get *I'm Turning On My PC, Now What?!* by Matthew James.

assessing options

Should you work in an office or at home? Some of the time or all of the time?

How many hours do you need to work? Think about it.
Are you looking for a job that will pay you the maximum dollars? That means you have to clear your schedule of other obligations so you can work all day, five days a week. Or perhaps you're willing to trade the dollars for extra free time so you can personally look after your kids or take care of an aging parent. Then you are headed for fewer hours a day or fewer days a week. Or do you need to work at your own pace, taking projects only when you want—or when a company needs you? Then you should consider freelance employment.

WORKING FIVE FULL DAYS A WEEK

Regular full-time employment: We're talking about 35 to 40 hours each workweek on the job (commonly 9 to 5, with a lunch break) in the office of your employer. The routine's steady, and the pay is too. And the perks add up; medium-sized and large firms offer health insurance (hospitalization and major medical, sometimes dental or vision coverage as well), disability, worker's compensation, paid vacation and sick leave, pensions, and assorted other goodies.

Telecommuting: Some firms allow an employee to work away from the office at least part of the time, staying in touch by e-mail. Such an arrangement can save commuting time and money. A firm may even set up their own computer connections and software to facilitate an employee's communication from a home office.

Flextime: Many companies allow full-time employees to stagger their work schedules. For instance, one person might prefer the conventional 9 to 5 routine, while an early bird works from 7:30 to 3:30, and someone else shows up at 10 and stays until 6.

WORKING LESS THAN FIVE DAYS A WEEK

Regular part-time: This is working in an office for anything less than 35 hours a week, either scheduled for a few hours each workday or for several full days a week. Prorated benefits may be offered if you work a minimum 17.5 hours.

Job Sharing: Two people share the responsibilities of a single job, although both work part-time. Perhaps one person works mornings and the other works afternoons. Or one works two days a week and the other works three. Careful coordination is key, so that the work is as seamless as if one person were doing it.

WORKING WHEN THE OCCASION ARISES

Temp work: Many firms offer short-term assignments, with no expectation of continued employment. You get paid—either by the company or by a temp agency—only for the days you're assigned to work. The temp agency may offer you benefits, depending on how many days you work during the year.

Consulting: You subcontract your services directly to a company or companies and charge them appropriate fees, which are usually spelled out in a contract. The companies pay you without withholding payroll taxes; you must file your taxes independently and arrange for your own health insurance, pension, and so on. You might work at home with occasional meetings at the firm, or you might be asked to do most of your work onsite. Warning: If your services are in great demand, you may end up working more hours than a full-timer. If they are not, you may need to return to a regular job.

NON-EXEMPT VS. EXEMPT

Non-Exempt: Entry-level and non-professional employees work for hourly wages (the federal minimum wage is $5.15 per hour). They get time-and-a-half for work in excess of 40 hours weekly (double time for weekends and holidays).

Exempt: Managerial and supervisory employees receive an annual salary. They work as many hours as needed to do their jobs without any extra pay for overtime.

responding to demand

What skills do employers prize above all?

There are skills that you can learn from working a job or taking classes, but there are other, less tangible skills that will endear you to a boss and ease your way up the career ladder. The best part is, you can develop most of them on your own.

Below is a list of skills highly favored by employers. Most everyone has learned a few of them, starting in kindergarten, because these are life skills as well as job skills. Concentrating on the ones you're already good at can impress prospective employers. Applying yourself to developing some of the others on the list enhances your value to a prospective employer.

TOP TEN SKILLS

1. Multitasking—doing several things simultaneously. For instance, can you talk on the phone, zap dinner in the microwave, and keep an eye on the news at the same time?

2. Prioritizing—performing tasks in order of their importance. Do you concentrate on getting your son to the dentist before working out when to pick up your dry cleaning?

3. Leading, directing, and motivating others—persuading people to participate in your plans and share your goals. Can you get friends to help clean out your basement so you all can have a party there?

4. Getting along with others and fostering teamwork—facilitating good relations among your colleagues. Do you seldom fight with loved ones? When you do fight, do you avoid ending an argument by not speaking to someone? If it sometimes does happen, do you try to clear up the misunderstanding within a day or two?

5. Communicating well—speaking and writing simply and clearly. Can friends always understand your notes and explanations or directions?

6. Handling pressure—functioning well in difficult situations. Do you remain calm and professional even when facing unreasonable deadlines?

7. Facility with numbers—using basic arithmetic easily and confidently. Can you balance your checkbook, or could you if you tried a bit harder?

8. Respecting hierarchy—adjusting to the conventions of a workplace. When you were in school, could you write papers the way your teacher wanted, even if you thought there were better ways?

9. Negotiating—practicing give-and-take to facilitate relationships and accomplish goals. If you go to the movies with a group, do you try to make a decision that everyone will be happy about?

10. Computer literacy—turning on the darn thing and cranking out a document. Have you at least learned the basics? Can you figure out simple stuff by trial and error?

sharpening skills

Never stop learning; it builds your marketable expertise

Most jobs have an educational requirement, and more and more these days, it's college. Why? Specific training aside, it's because having graduated from college shows an employer that you can finish what you've started and that you are seriously interested in a career with a future. That said, knowledge acquired on the job or through life experiences or from volunteering may possibly outweigh your lack of specific training or education for a position.

How do you know if you have the education you'll need for the job you want? Talk to people in the field you're considering and ask about their academic achievements. If you determine that you do need more schooling, set about filling in the blanks. Take courses at night, in correspondence school or through an online program, or attend professional seminars, or enroll in a program that leads to a technical certification.

The same goes for people on the job. Not keeping skills sharp is the biggest mistake actively employed people make. How do you know if you are sliding on the skill scale? Look at your work over the past five years. If you see that you haven't learned any new ways of doing business—or doing it better—you may need more education.

Don't have the time or money, you say? No one does, so make some sacrifices. Education is an investment that will pay off. And smart workers often find ways to hone their skills by having their companies help them. Did you know that many corporations employing 50 people or more help pay for college or graduate school? Most are happy to hear that employees want to attend industry conferences, lectures, or seminars, and will give time—and sometimes money—to do it.

WHAT'S OUT THERE: EDUCATION

Whether you prefer learning in-house (on company time), off-site (check the firm's policy on tuition reimbursement), or at home (on your computer), these days you can find something to suit your taste, your wallet, and your lifestyle.

Continuing Education Courses: Offered by your local high schools, community colleges, and universities, these courses generally target specific skills (auto mechanics, Word 2000, beginning Italian) and do not lead to a degree.

Degree Programs: Classes at a college or university leading to a degree or certificate. They can be attended either full-time, evenings, or weekends.

Seminars: One-day or one-week courses are offered on a host of business topics. The American Management Association's Web site (www.amanet.org) offers a comprehensive selection. Listings by topic can be found at www.seminarfinder.com. For listings by state, look at www.seminarinfo.com.

Correspondence Courses: Excellent resources are the University Continuing Education Association site at www.nucea.edu as well as www.lifelonglearning.com or www.petersons.com. Check out both print and online courses, and information on available scholarships and grants.

Degrees at a Distance: Most universities offer courses online now. Click on a university's Web site to learn about offerings. Also see listings of over 200,000 online courses by searching www.virtual.net.uy/netvicourses.html or www.aln.org/coursedirectory, or even the major search engines such as www.lycos.com.

rating experience

It's almost always crucial in landing a job. But there are creative ways to use it— or the lack of it

You are your job experiences. They have shaped you for better or worse. Sure, you should match your experiences as closely as you can to the job you want. But what if you don't have any job history that applies? Experiences gained through volunteer activities, internships, or special school activities are fair game. Experience is experience is experience, whether you've been paid for it or not.

An important challenge in considering your history is to review the good and the bad elements—the promotions and the terminations, the great job you did and the not-so-hot project, the boss who loved you and the one who didn't. Weave these different threads into a colorful tapestry that inspires prospective employers to consider you as someone they just have to hire.

In fact, you can take your history a step further by focusing on sterling moments in your career so far—how your sincerity and persuasiveness changed the customer's mind and saved the account; how your ideas about doing things differently brought the project in ahead of schedule; how you replaced two people and boosted production statistics for the month. You will need to think about your failures too, and consider what you learned from them.

Then there's the inevitable area where you have no experience whatsoever. Don't be discouraged; no one has everything that a job description calls for or an employer seeks. Some accommodation is customary between the ideal the company envisions and the actual candidates who present themselves to be interviewed.

If you are enthusiastic about learning on the job and can draw parallels with instances where you have picked up new information quickly, you can overcome gaps in your work history. Adaptability is not just a skill, it's another aspect of your job experience.

STEP BY STEP: GETTING EXPERIENCE

1. Volunteer to do an unpaid or low-paid internship for a short period of time in the field in which you want to gain experience. Not-for-profit organizations welcome free labor and may give you the opportunity to learn and develop your skills. Then you can say with honesty that you have worked as a salesperson, interviewer, data entry clerk, programmer, conference planner, or fund-raiser.

2. Temp in the field you want. Ask for a job that puts you in proximity to a position for which you seek experience. Often your busy employer won't mind if you, the eager temporary assistant, take over some of the more routine tasks she has to do, and gradually you can learn at least a few of the skills you need for a job such as hers.

3. Talk to people in the field you are interested in to find out how they got started. Often a specific field has entry-level positions created to give neophytes such as yourself on-the-job training.

HOW TO VOLUNTEER

Volunteering is the fastest and most effective way to gain experience. Check out these Web sites.
   www.4work.com
   www.idealist.org
   www.volunteermatch.org
   www.councilexchanges.org

Call these organizations for information on where to go and whom to call.
1 800 VOLUNTEER
1 888 77YOUTH

FIRST PERSON   **SUCCESS STORY**

Making a connection

Robert J., a placement officer for paralegal students, wanted to use his abilities to get a better-paying position. He heard about a job as an employment interviewer in a medical school, and went to meet with the employment manager. During their talk Robert convinced his prospective boss that placing graduate students in law firms and identifying suitable candidates for medical positions called for similar skills: listening well, probing for information, sizing up people quickly, and matching people to jobs that suited them. He got the job, and by translating those skills that he had used in his work before, Robert was able to ease his learning curve in the new field.

Robert J., Steubenville, Ohio

now what do I do?

Answers to common problems

I have spent the last ten years at home, raising my children. Now I want to work outside the home. Where do I start?

This is one of the most frequently asked questions these days. First you need to figure out your most marketable skills. Budgeting? Raising money for charities? Motivating others? Writing computer programs? List these skills, along with tasks you've performed while working as a volunteer for school, church, or a charity. Then think about jobs you could do that would capitalize on these experiences.

Next, consider the skills you lack. Set about acquiring them through self-directed or group study. Network with every acquaintance you have and meet with people who have jobs that interest you. Ask if you can follow them around for a few hours to get live, up-to-the-minute exposure to their workplace and the skills they use. Consider getting an internship or an entry-level job (see Chapter 4) in the industry or profession you like, and working your way up. Your maturity, dedication, and perseverance will often impress employers and lead to advancement.

How do I know if I'm going to like a job before I start doing it?

You don't. That's why it's often said that experience is the best teacher. All you can do is guess, based on what you know about your interests, work style, and ambitions. You can hope you've made a good choice, but you'll never know for sure until you try. But interviewing people in the field and taking courses in related subjects can help.

Will my age—64—count against me?

Not if you keep up your skills, especially in the computer area. Don't let yourself get outdated. Strive to be adaptable, welcome change, and embrace new ways of doing things as well as new people to do them with. And keep on learning and studying and exploring. Also, expect to be recognized for the advantages you offer as an older worker—stability, judgment, experience—and no emergency child-care problems.

I'm 22 and have no idea what I want to do with my life. Where do I start?

Don't worry. Few at age 22 ever know what they want to do with themselves. Start by giving serious thought to your innate abilities, your preferences for work environment, what you'd like to accomplish in the short and long term. Don't forget to talk to people who know you well about their perceptions of your abilities. Temping is a good option if you really are lost—it will plunge you right into a work environment, and you'll quickly see what you like and don't like in different types of industries.

I'm disabled but am willing and eager to work. How should I go about it?

Enthusiasm is key. Depending on your disability, you might profit from going to a rehabilitation center and taking advantage of their assessment services. Such centers usually can offer you training in specific skills and, sometimes, an opportunity to be presented to a business advisory committee of employers. You will be given help with your resumé and general presentation, and offered the chance to make business contacts and connections.

HELPFUL RESOURCES

WEB ADDRESSES AND CONTACTS	PUBLICATIONS
www.jobfindersonline.com	**Professional's Job Finder** by Daniel Lauber
www.careers.org	
www.aarp.org/working_options/home.html/	**Jobs and Careers with Non-Profit Organizations** by Dr. Ronald Krannich
	100 Jobs in Social Change by Harley Jebens
	How to Survive and Prosper As an Artist By Carroll Michels

Resumés

Putting your life on paper 30
It's your passport to a new job

Parts of the whole 32
Concentrate on one section at a time

Organizing for effect 34
Lead with your strong suit

Tailoring your track record 36
Fit your work history to the job you want

Emphasizing strengths 38
Look at experience through job functions

A resumé without jobs 40
Put life experience to work for you

Electronic resumé 42
Show off your computer skills at the same time

Writing cover letters 44
Focus the recruiter's attention

Customizing letters 46
Answer job requirements step-by-step

Now what do I do? 48
Answers to common problems

A resumé sums up who you are in the workforce—
where you've been, what you've done, and when you did it.

putting your life on paper

Tough as it is to do, a good resumé can be your passport to a more satisfying job

Commit the essence of your working life to one flimsy sheet of paper? Impossible! No wonder you feel so nervous when you think about it. What to put in? What to leave out? How much detail?

A resumé sums up who you are in the workforce—where you've been, what you've done, and when you did it. More important, it should prompt an interviewer to ask you why you've done what you've done. That's what interviewers live for—probing the deep, dark recesses of your psyche. They hope to unearth an inner force driving you toward the very job they have available. If your resumé points to that job, the interviewer will work hard to discover the reasons why you're a perfect fit for it.

The principal components of a resumé are your prior accomplishments—on the job, in school, even at home and in the community. Among those accomplishments recruiters want to find are evidence of your sterling attributes, such as whether you're a creative thinker, a hard worker, a reliable individual. They may want to see if you've held progressively responsible positions, worked well independently and/or as part of a team, and learn what honors and awards you've earned along the way.

As you work out the best way to describe your accomplishments on your resumé, you will gain a better understanding of the advantages you can offer an employer—which in turn will contribute to a more convincing interview.

RESUMÉ WRITING TIPS

In a resumé, clarity of expression is paramount. After all, recruiters are a busy bunch; if your resumé isn't easy to read, they won't waste time trying. Here are some tips that can improve the odds that your resumé will be read:

➤ Use crisp phrases, starting with action verbs (past tense for former jobs, present tense for your current job) when describing your work.

➤ Describe actual accomplishments rather than generalizing about your duties. "Streamlined operations, resulting in 30% increase in productivity" works much better than "Managed operations."

➤ Structure all the entries in a similar way. Each entry needs a job title, name of company, dates of employment, and one or more accomplishments. Arrange these components in exactly the same way for each entry. Consistency helps to clarify.

➤ Work for precision. Every word counts, whether you're squeezing one year—or ten, twenty, or thirty years—into a page or two. Take time to search for just the right word to describe your unique attributes and experiences.

parts of the whole

Help the reader go through your resumé one step at a time

When you sit down to design your resumé, you first need to decide how to organize your material. Typically the major headings are Experience, Education, and Skills.

EXPERIENCE

This major section of your resumé covers your working history. If you decide to go with the traditional chronological form, start with your most recent job and work backwards (up to ten years).

If you want to sort your working history by function, you will need to analyze your experience (job and/or life) according to the abilities and skills you have mastered, or by your accomplishments. You may want to leave out some things you have done, to concentrate on the skills relevant to the job you want. (More specific information about exactly how to work out these two formats can be found on pages 36-39.)

EDUCATION

List your schools and degrees, certificates or diplomas, beginning with the first degree earned. Add honors such as cum laude (graduated with honor) or Phi Beta Kappa. If you're looking for a technical job, a summary of related college courses is expected. Never put down a degree you haven't earned; if you are lacking a thesis or a few hours' coursework, spell that out. If you've been out of school for longer than 10 years, leave off the dates.

The section on education usually appears at the end of your resumé, but it might be placed at the top if you've just graduated from college and you went to a school that's much admired. The idea is, hit them hard with Harvard, but edge Podunk Community College down toward the end of the page.

SKILLS

At the end of your resumé list computer programs and types of computer hardware you have worked on, in addition to foreign languages in which you are adept and other special abilities you have developed.

OPTIONAL RESUMÉ SECTIONS

OBJECTIVE

This is a statement at the top of your resumé about the kind of job you want. It lets a recruiter know your aim, but it could limit the jobs for which you are considered.

SUMMARY OF QUALIFICATIONS

This brief listing, also at the top of a resumé, highlights your strongest selling points relating to the job you want. Unless your resumé is short, or your jobs have been in different fields, this information may be more effective in your cover letter.

VOLUNTEER ACTIVITIES

Here's where you can showcase serious commitment to working in your community—coaching a Little League team, organizing an art show at the local museum, reading to the blind, or tutoring disadvantaged students. Volunteer jobs are important because they show that you are building skills that can apply to a paid job.

INTERESTS

This entry describes hobbies and favorite leisure-time activities. "Playing the flute, traveling abroad, singing in the choir," provides a conversation starter. But don't go overboard; two to four interests will do. Put it at the end of the resumé.

organizing for effect

(see page 36 for more detail)

*Lead with
information
that showcases
the best you have
to offer*

For most job seekers, a chronological list of previous jobs is just fine (see page 36 for more detail). However, if you have bounced from job to job, you're changing fields, or you have little work experience, you may want to consider organizing your resumé by the functions you have performed, whether at a job, in volunteer work, or in some other venue.

A good plan might be to develop both chronological and functional resumés and study the effectiveness of each type for your own work history. Show both to friends and to mentors—those more experienced associates who are willing to advise you about your career. Their preferences can steer you toward the format best suited for you.

Whichever type you compose, tailor it to the particular position you want, emphasizing accomplishments that best fit the job's requirements. This could mean you'll need to write several resumés in order to apply for various jobs. You may even need to customize a resumé for an unusual job. Tough sledding? Sure, but it's sledding that may enable you to work at something you really want to do.

KEEP IT ACTIVE

Using "to be" verbs, such as "was," "is," "were," or "are," sound much too passive. Instead, use active verbs. They'll add a little muscle to your page. Right away you sound more dynamic.

Examples of Active Verbs Found on Effective Resumés

anticipated	facilitated	pinpointed
applied	framed	planned
audited	guided	presented
analyzed	hosted	processed
broadened	identified	provided
built	implemented	quantified
consolidated	improved	reduced
channeled	initiated	remedied
conceived	inventoried	revamped
coordinated	joined	selected
customized	launched	spearheaded
devised	maintained	steered
developed	modeled	supervised
designed	modified	tabulated
directed	negotiated	tightened
effected	neutralized	undertook
estimated	organized	validated
evaluated	performed	widened

SECRET FOR A GREAT RESUMÉ

Revise, revise, revise (oh, dreaded word!). Keep on refining your resume during the job-hunting process. Before every interview, tailor a resume to the job you are applying for. Then after the interview, edit it again, based on what you learned. Yes, it's grueling. Yes, it's tedious. But it's one of the keys to job-hunting success.

tailoring a track record

When your job history tells a story that leads directly to the job you want

Chronological resumés, by far the most popular kind, re-create your past work and educational history step-by-step. The main advantage: an interviewer can grasp where you are today and how far you've come. The major disadvantage: chronology can shift the emphasis from what you want to do to what you have done and for how long. For this reason, it is important that the descriptions of your duties in each job are compelling. (Read "Resumé Writing Tips" on page 31 before starting to write.)

A—An Objective is not necessary, but it may help if you have a career plan in mind. You might want to use it to lead off your cover letter instead.

B—The Summary can help the interviewer zoom in on your strengths, but the cover letter may be a better place to present them.

C—List jobs in reverse order, beginning with the most recent. In a chronological resumé, jobs should lead progressively nearer to your stated objective (this may require a second page).

D—Try to show positive results that you achieved for the company.

E—Active verbs can help you demonstrate how innovative and proactive you are in each and every work situation.

F—Point out any extra study you have done that would hone your professional skills.

Katherine Knight
55 Hilltop Crest
Albany, NY 10507

knight@koolmail.com
(215) 555-7250

(A) OBJECTIVE: Position as Editor of Business Publications

(B) SUMMARY: Advanced editorial skills, accomplished at helping business executives express themselves more fluently, innovative at delivering books on time and within budget.

(C) EXPERIENCE:

1999 - Present   Associate Editor, BusinessFirst Press

Edit eight books annually for business readers. Specialize in helping professionals in every field develop writing skills.

(D) Supervise book development projects, moving from raw manuscript through press delivery, and manage a budget in low six figures for each. Trimmed costs saving an average of $15,000/book.

1994 - 1998   Supervisor, Document Production, J.R. Finnegan, Esq.

Implemented glossary of legal terms for use by freelance proofreaders in legal office turning out 200 documents/week.

Revised scheduling of legal proofreaders in order to employ graduate students with superior language skills, saving $35,000/year.

1990 - 1994   High School English teacher, Milwaukee Public Schools

(E) Wrote handbook for laboratory designed to help high school seniors learn the basics of real-life banking, investing, and insurance.

Taught business writing and created standardized lesson plans for courses in the subject to be used by new teachers.

EDUCATION: College of the Mountains, B.A. History, 1990. National Merit Finalist

Business Editor for College Newspaper, 2 years

(F) Correspondence courses in editing business writing, NY State College at Albany

OTHER SKILLS: Fluent in Spanish
Proficient in Word, Excel, QuarkXpress, Publisher 99

VOLUNTEER ACTIVITIES:
Tutor for Growing Great Readers, which aids Hispanic children with reading problems.

INTERESTS, HOBBIES:
Swimming, scubadiving, reading Civil War history

emphasizing strengths

When your qualifications are stronger than your job history

Functional resumés put emphasis on what you have done rather than when and where you've done it. Their main advantage is that they highlight skills—a particular advantage if you're changing careers or have jumped around a lot among different industries and positions. Their main disadvantage is that they can make it difficult for an interviewer to reconstruct your experience in the customary chronological way. To make it easier for a prospective employer to read, give a summary of your job history at the end.

A—Because you may be changing fields, clearly identify the job you are seeking.

B—Pick out the skills needed for the job you want, and show how your experience in other fields is applicable.

C—Briefly summarize—bare facts only—your work history chronologically.

D—Having taken courses or seminars in the field you want to try demonstrates your motivation and interest.

E—Don't forget those extras. You may get a break because a firm just took on a new Spanish client or needs someone who knows how to work their Quark program for the in-house newsletter. Or they may have just acquired a sports account.

KATHERINE KNIGHT

55 Hilltop Crest
Albany, NY 10507

knight@koolmail.com
(215) 555-7250

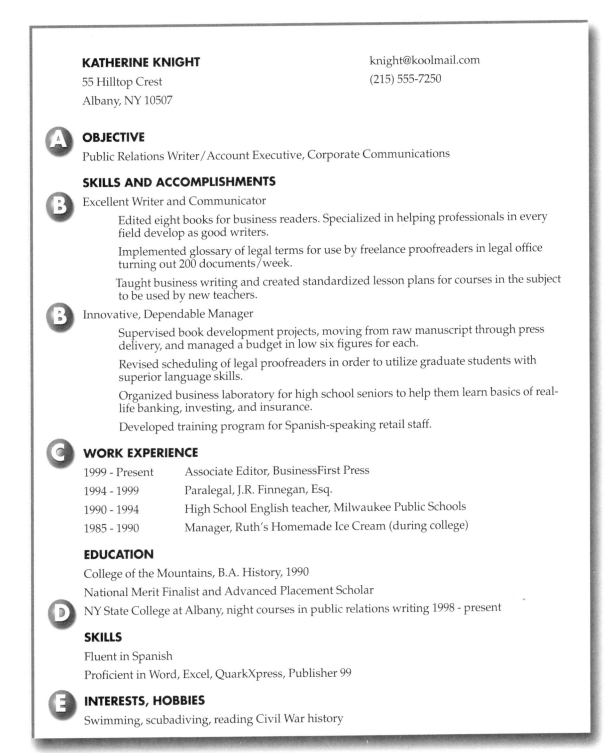

A OBJECTIVE

Public Relations Writer/Account Executive, Corporate Communications

SKILLS AND ACCOMPLISHMENTS

B Excellent Writer and Communicator

Edited eight books for business readers. Specialized in helping professionals in every field develop as good writers.

Implemented glossary of legal terms for use by freelance proofreaders in legal office turning out 200 documents/week.

Taught business writing and created standardized lesson plans for courses in the subject to be used by new teachers.

B Innovative, Dependable Manager

Supervised book development projects, moving from raw manuscript through press delivery, and managed a budget in low six figures for each.

Revised scheduling of legal proofreaders in order to utilize graduate students with superior language skills.

Organized business laboratory for high school seniors to help them learn basics of real-life banking, investing, and insurance.

Developed training program for Spanish-speaking retail staff.

C WORK EXPERIENCE

1999 - Present	Associate Editor, BusinessFirst Press
1994 - 1999	Paralegal, J.R. Finnegan, Esq.
1990 - 1994	High School English teacher, Milwaukee Public Schools
1985 - 1990	Manager, Ruth's Homemade Ice Cream (during college)

EDUCATION

College of the Mountains, B.A. History, 1990

National Merit Finalist and Advanced Placement Scholar

D NY State College at Albany, night courses in public relations writing 1998 - present

SKILLS

Fluent in Spanish

Proficient in Word, Excel, QuarkXpress, Publisher 99

E INTERESTS, HOBBIES

Swimming, scubadiving, reading Civil War history

a resumé without jobs

When you're just out of college, or entering the job market after a long absence

Yes, everybody really does find a first job, despite having no experience. Whether you've been out of the marketplace for years, or you're looking for your first crack at it, you will find a spot. It is just a matter of putting together a resumé that points out accomplishments in every part of your life. After all, life experience is valid experience, and can be helpful in finding a spot to start.

A—If you are a recent graduate and you were a high achiever, lead with that. If not, this area might be valuable if you went to a fine school or have recently attended professional seminars in the field you want to enter. Otherwise, put EDUCATION and attendant honors at the bottom of the page.

B—Summer jobs and an unsalaried internship indicate your willingness to learn and your capacity for hard work.

C—Volunteer activities help to present you as an innovative, take-charge person if you describe duties and accomplishments that could be valuable in the workplace.

D—You can often get a foot in the door with a special ability.

E—Many entry-level jobs require computer skills.

KATHERINE KNIGHT   knight@koolmail.com
55 Hilltop Crest   (215) 555-7250
College Town, NY 10507

(A) EDUCATION

College of the Mountains, B.A. History, GPA 3.3, May 2000

HONORS

National Merit Finalist and Advanced Placement Scholar

(B) WORK EXPERIENCE

Corporate Paralegal (Internship)
Darrow & Sons   Summer 1999

Lifeguard/Swim Coach
Minnewaska Golf Club   Summers 1996 - 1998

VOLUNTEER ACTIVITIES

(C)
President, Vice President, Co-Founder
50-member Native-American Student Union   1995 - 1999
• Drafted constitution; oversaw budget allocation
        process, promotions;
• Coordinated events to foster appreciation of
        Native-American history and culture.

Disk Jockey—Student Volunteer
WCOL—Campus Radio Station   1997 - 1999
• Developed and maintained volunteers' schedules

Ruraltown Day Care Center   1998 - 2000
(for underprivileged children)
• Instituted cross-referenced billing records to facilitate
        late-payment reminders

SKILLS: (D) Excellent Writer and Communicator
                Fluent in written and oral Spanish
(E) Proficient in Word, Excel, QuarkXpress, Publisher 99

INTERESTS: Professional Swimmer, avid reader

electronic resumé

Now that computers have taken over every aspect of our twenty-first century lives (and we thought it would be robots!), you might want to factor them into your job search. If you are proficient at using the Internet (home of the Web)—and particularly if you are aiming for a high-tech job—sending an e-resumé is a good idea.

Don't worry if you've never done it before. Transmitting your resumé through a computer is hardly rocket science if you are already using the computer to write your resumé and you are familiar with e-mail. All you need to do is convert your resumé to a text version that can be read on any computer. "Plain" text is usually safest, and is often called for in job ads. Other names used for plain text are ASCII, Text Only, or DOS text. Essentially, plain text gets rid of italics, bullets, and all your fancy formatting, so that your resumé can be read by any computer.

STEP BY STEP: CONVERT YOUR RESUMÉ TO PLAIN TEXT

1. Open your resumé document.
2. Select "Save as," and rename the file "resume.plaintext,"
3. Save as "plaintext" or "text only."

Look at this new plaintext document. You will note that the format has been simplified—no bold-face type, no underlining, no bullets, no italics.

Now that you know how your resumé will look when it is sent by e-mail, you may want to spruce it up with judicious use of capital letters and indents. Here are some suggestions:

1. For bullets, substitute asterisks, plus signs, or dashes.
2. For underlining text, try using all-capital letters instead.
3. For separating sections, a line of dashes or asterisks can serve.
4. For bold type or special fonts, use all-capital letters or set off the phrase with asterisks or plus signs.

It's best to skip most other formatting devices, because they might possibly transmit as unreadable symbols. If any such symbols show up in your plain-text resumé, remove them. Then proofread the e-resumé a final time.

ASK THE EXPERTS

Should I send a hard copy of my resumé?

It's a good practice to follow up your e-resumé by sending a hard copy by snail mail (U.S. Postal Service). This may seem repetitious, but it's good insurance. And a beautifully-formatted resumé printed in a clear, black font on white or creamy 20-pound bond paper is always very impressive.

What is an electronic form?

An e-form is created by a job board Web site. By inputting information about your job history in the blanks provided on the form, you produce an e-resumé that is accessible by viewers of the site.

When should I use electronic forms or post my resumé?

Never, if you are concerned about confidentiality. If you are still working, people at your company may notice your resumé on a Web site. And your address and phone number may be accessed by thousands on such sites. (Consider renting a post office box and opening a voice mail account if you post on a Web site).

WHAT'S OUT THERE

Web Addresses

www.eresumes.com
Rebecca Smith's online guide includes a step-by-step tutorial

www.dbm.com/jobguide
The Riley Guide

Publications

Electronic Resumés and Online Networking: How to Use the Web to Do a Better Job Search
by Rebecca Smith, Career Press

The Guide to Internet Job Searching
by Margaret Riley-Dikel and Frances Roehm, VGM Career Horizons

writing cover letters

Draw the interviewer's attention to your strengths

In olden days, job applicants sent handwritten notes along with their resumés. The prospective employer could thus marvel at their fine script while observing the form and flow of their prose. Although assessing penmanship is no longer in style, the cover letter—now computer generated—survives. Be forewarned: a resumé that dares to stand without one is like a ship without an anchor—drifting from here to there without ever being able to land at its destination.

The main purpose of a cover letter, then and now, is to direct the prospective employer's eye to the key features of your resumé. It can also add points not immediately evident in your resumé, such as your special qualifications for the job you are writing about.

Consider the different ways to compose the letter. You can match the job's requisites point for point with your capabilities. Or you can summarize your qualifications and background, and discuss why you're the one for the job. Or you can simply introduce yourself briefly and pleasantly, refer to the job in question, and indicate your availability and contact numbers.

But above all, be clear. Pare down the letter until it is concise and to the point. Also, be sure to refer specifically to the position in question and how you heard of it. Remember, the prospective employer may have advertised ten different jobs at the same time.

Never, never send a photocopy or a form cover letter. You can develop a generic body to your cover letter that can be used over and over, but each time you send it out, you should make slight modifications that refer to the actual job you want. *Customizing each letter is imperative.* You want to show the prospective employer that you've spent some time and effort thinking about how you might fit into that job of theirs.

**"I'm a fast learner...
I have knowlege of word procesing...
You won't be disappointed."**

Vague, empty words, with typos. Cite your
specific strengths and real skills.

**"I'm applying for
the job you advertised."**

Where? When? Which one of 7? Always reference
the date of the ad you are responding to and the job
title mentioned in the ad.

**"I need a job, any job.
Please help me. Now!"**

Desperate and unfocused. You want to focus on
how you can contribute to the company,
not on how they need to help you.

**"My last supervisor
had went to a seminar..."**

Ungrammatical. Not proofread, and careless.
Have a friend proofread your letters.

"Hey, I'm the man."

Hardly. Cut out all cute phrases, slang, condescension.
Remember, finding the right person is a serious business for the recruiter.
It has to be equally serious for you, unless you're
applying for a disc jockey spot at a rock station.

Whether you realize it or not, tricky phrases come across to most readers as efforts on your part to cover up your anxieties.
Instead, simply put your trust in straightforward, businesslike communication.

customizing letters

Standard format
for cover letter

123 Main Street
Excelsior, NY 10703
January 3, 2001

Joan R. Fine, VP
Garber College
695 Clay Avenue
Excelsior, NY 10705

Refer to
where you
heard about
the job

Re: Career Development Director
● (*The Excelsior Times*, December 29, 2000)

Dear Ms. Fine:

For most of my career as a personnel officer, I have been heavily involved in directing college relations. At my last position, I identified colleges whose students my firm pursued via job fairs, on-site interviewing, advertising, and hosted events on campus. I also handled all career counseling duties for our employees.

A Review
relevant
experience

I am now seeking a position as a career development director. My strengths are knowledge of the job market and workplace realities, a network of contacts with area employers and organizations, and an easy rapport with my colleagues.

B Sum up
special abilities
that fit the job
requirements

I hope to meet with you soon to discuss the above position in more detail. Please feel free to call me at my home number 447-9772, or contact me at my e-mail address grock@argent.com.

C Mention
where you
can be
easily
reached

Sincerely,

George Rockford

I believe my knowledge, skills, and abilities provide a perfect match for the job you have advertised (*The Excelsior Times*, December 29, 2000). The job requires....., I offer....

job requires....	I offer...
• 10 years relevant experience	• 12 years in insurance
• Excellent writing skills, work in marketing communications, research newsletters	• 2 years experience writing corporate brochures
• Detail-oriented coordinator, multitasker, good follow-up	• Skills I have developed in 8 years of claims investigation

Delete paragraph End with paragraph

I believe my accomplishments and strengths provide a perfect match for the job you have advertised (The Excelsior Times, December 29, 2000). My major accomplishments are:

• Met department's goals and objectives without exceeding budgeted expenses, despite downsizing of staff from 4 to 2.

• Reorganized department's billing procedures, resulting in 25% increase in receivables last year.

• Won Best Employee of the Year in 2000.

My major strengths are:

• Reputation as a problem solver with ability to promote consensus in order to build and lead a strong team.

• Superior oral and written communication skills: guest speaker at industry association meetings; President of Co-op Board; Editor of PTA bulletin.

• Upbeat, proactive person with a good sense of humor.

Delete paragraph End with paragraph

now what do I do?

Answers to common problems

How long should my resumé be?

If you've worked for more than fifteen years, you can go for two pages; otherwise get it all on a single page. Academics are allowed—indeed, expected—to append a list of all publications. Creative types can list awards and honors.

What if I'm changing careers?

Don't try to hide anything. Focus on your transferable assets: skills that would be useful in the new field, a good work ethic, responsible habits, reliability, and productivity demonstrated throughout your previous career. Don't ignore work you've done as a volunteer, a temp, or an unpaid intern as a way of building up experience and credentials in your new field.

Should I call a company to follow up after sending in my resumé?

If it's a big firm, say, over 200 people, be prepared for a lot of curt answers, hangups, and rejections if you do. Personnel staff in high-volume employment divisions won't stop to search for your resumé in the piles that have come in. They'll tell you to wait for a call or postcard. However, every once in a while in smaller firms you just may call at the right moment and get a receptive person who is willing to help. But if you are demanding, she may remember your name for the wrong reason.

I've been downsized in my last few jobs. Prospective employers seem to assume I've been job-hopping and I don't get many calls to interview.

In this case, add a line to each job description about why you left, such as: "Left due to company reorganization."

Must I include my GPA?

No, not if it's 3.0 (B average) or under. And it isn't really called for unless you are a recent graduate. Then, if it's significantly higher in your major, include that information: "3.2 GPA; 3.6 in major." List all honors, awards, and scholarships, too.

I took off two years to do volunteer work in South America. Employers seem to think I'm unstable or something.

Treat the work abroad as though it were another job by stressing the skills you gained in the interim. In your cover letter, describe how your voluntary hiatus from the workplace has enriched you personally and made you more productive. But do state your determination to return to a more conventional life.

How about unusual colors, format, or presentation for the resumé?

Play it safe, be conservative, no blue paper, curlicues, flowers, or gothic fonts. Stick with a good grade of paper, white or cream, with a businesslike font, for both resumé and letter. That way, you can't lose. Save the resumé disguised as a fortune cookie in a box, or scrolled, rolled, and tied with a ribbon for graphic design firms, the creative side of publishing, or advertising agencies that are usually (but not always) less stuffy.

HELPFUL RESOURCES

WEB ADDRESSES	PUBLICATIONS
www.latimes.com	**CareerXroads** by Gerry Crispin and Mark Mehler "Internet Resources"
www.monster.com	
www.nytimes.com	**Last Minute Resumés** by Brandon Toropov
www.washingtonpost.com	**Proven Resumés** by Regina Pontow
	Ready to Go Resumés by Yana Parker

Job resources

Print ads 52
Most companies rely on them

On-line ads 54
A fast-growing job resource

Career services 56
Alumni associations and professional groups

Employment agencies 58
Putting you in the job picture

Headhunters 60
Specialists in executive jobs

Research 62
Boning up on companies and jobs

Keeping on track 64
Don't depend on memory alone

Now what do I do? 66
Answers to common problems

1 2 3 4 5 6 7 8 9

All sorts of organizations either specialize in
job searches or have job-search sections that help you make
valuable contacts, both online and off.

print ads

One 20-word ad may hold the key to your future.

Great, you've got your resumé together. Now you need to look at what's available in the marketplace. Start by studying the classifieds, or "want ads," in the local newspaper or the newspaper that serves the nearest large city. Also check to see if there are other classified sections for jobs in different parts of the Sunday paper, for example, in the business section or education section.

And don't forget to look for ads in major professional and trade publications. (See page 57, "Other Associations to Contact.")

Aside from information about current job openings and where to apply, you'll find that by reading the classifieds you can familiarize yourself with some of the jargon particular to an industry or a profession. Roam through the ads and you may even discover attractive jobs you had never previously considered!

Responding to classified ads has recently been considered a less effective tactic for a job search than other methods, such as working the Internet or depending solely on personal contacts. But check the ads anyway; most companies continue to invest big dollars advertising their job openings in print, as do employment agencies. At the very least, you will generate interviews, which will give you practice for the main event.

DIFFERENT TYPES OF PRINT ADS

THE CLASSIFIEDS

Also known as help-wanted ads, they are listed alphabetically according to position (i.e., "accountant" before "bookkeeper"). Some are as elaborate as a letter, others are pure shorthand. Most describe briefly the available position and suggest how to respond.

THE LOW-END AD

This is an inexpensive ad, run probably by the company itself, but possibly by an employment agency (agencies do not always identify themselves as such). This is also known as a blind ad—the company and address are not identified. Reasons for running a blind ad might be that the company seeks to fill a position that's currently occupied, or it doesn't want its employees (or competitors) to know of its search for prospects.

Responding to a blind ad has drawbacks. You don't know where you're sending your resumé; you could be applying to your own company (!) or a company you would never ordinarily consider. The salary for a position in a bare-bones ad is probably not as high as those described in more elaborate ads.

THE HIGH-END AD

Display ads with special borders, backgrounds, and typefaces are larger, more elaborate, and cost a pretty penny too. You can assume the company has some resources if it runs a display ad in a major metropolitan newspaper. Higher-paying professional positions are usually featured in display ads. They stand out in the tightly-woven text of the run-of-the-mill classified sections.

JOIN US!

NEW OFFICE OPENING

Well-known Hotel has the following positions available:

- Comptroller Manager
- Operations Manager Assistant
- Coffee Shop Manager
- Customer Service Coordinator

Fax resumé

GROW WITH US!

Are you energetic? A self-starter? A go getter?

Smythe, Rigsby & Baker, a fast-paced advertising firm, is expanding. We are seeking dynamic candidates with excellent decision-making skills. Entry level positions available in Human Resources, Sales, and Accounting.

New graduates welcome
Fax resumé and salary requirements

on-line ads

Tune in, turn on, and the world's at your doorstep

The good news is that there are currently an estimated 50,000 Web sites devoted to job search, career advice, and resumé building. On many of them, you can post your resumé for free. Most newspapers nowadays post job listings from their classified section on their own Web site. Government agencies have sites complete with job listings, and there are sites devoted to different specialties: techie sites, lawyer sites, human resources sites, college grad sites, and so on.

If you have a specific career or location picked out, explore membership association sites. A guide to these sites can be found at American Society of Association Executives, *www.asaenet.org* by clicking on their "Find associations" and then "Gateway to Associations." If you want a job as a physician's assistant, look for the American Academy of Physician's Assistants. Hoping for something in public relations? See the Public Relations Society of America. Want to use your language skills? Try the American Translators Association.

These sites and others offer job leads and up-to-date information on the latest trends in many fields. Locate an industry-specific discussion list like HRNet (Web site: *listserv@cornell.edu*) or trdevl-l (Web site: *listserv@lists.psu.edu*) to talk to practitioners and academics. Or "**lurk**" (read information from on-line discussions without responding yourself) and take notes on the issues that absorb people in your chosen field.

A word of warning: e-mail can change the format of your resumé, or turn it into a gobbledegook of coding symbols. Before sending your resumé electronically, refer back to pages 42-43 in Chapter 2 to be sure that it is formatted correctly for transmittal.

SK THE EXPERTS

Is it okay to e-mail my resumé to professional associations, agencies, career columnists, or career Web sites without asking?

Rather than just sending it without asking, it's better to first ascertain whether the person at the other end is willing to look over your resumé, make comments, and maybe refer it to someone with hiring responsibilities. If so, your e-mail message should be the equivalent of a good general cover letter. State your strengths and suitability, ask for advice or consideration, and attach your resumé.

Is it a good idea to post my resumé on a job Web site?

The main issue here is confidentiality. Anyone could access your resumé and deduce that you are in the market for a new job—including your current boss! However, if you're not currently employed, posting can increase your chances of being discovered. Research the job site first and determine if it is visited by companies you would like to work for. Also consider renting a post office box and hiring an answering service so your personal address and phone number will not be exposed.

Do companies ever list jobs on their Web site?

Yes, many of them do. If you are interested in working for a particular company, or for a government agency or non-profit group in your area, go to the organization's Web site. On the home page, look for links with names such as "Job Postings," "Careers," or "Employment Opportunities."

career services

Your alma mater may still be there for you

Sometimes overlooked, but very effective, are job placement services run by colleges, universities, and technical and business schools for their alumni and students. These services often include testing, counseling, help with your resumé, leads on jobs and internships, and seminars on job search tactics. Some have computerized databases that automatically match resumés to job openings and mail copies to prospective employers.

And that's not all. Most school placement services post the information they receive about job openings on bulletin boards, in newsletters, or on their Web sites. They also schedule interviewing days on campus or participate in career fairs, where corporate recruiters come to meet graduating students or alumni.

A major advantage: often jobs listed with college job placement services are not being advertised elsewhere. The employer may favor the college because he himself is an alumnus, or because he's had good luck hiring there.

Even if you've been out of school for a few years—or a bunch—check with your alumni association. Special-interest clubs at the college—the French Circle, say, or the Physics Club—may also provide links to opportunities in your career of choice, especially if the college's department is well-respected.

OTHER ASSOCIATIONS TO CONTACT

All sorts of organizations either specialize in job searches or have job-search sections that help you make valuable contacts, both on-line and off. Here are sources that can give you leads and support. To reach any of the organizations mentioned here, check the phone book to see if there are chapters or offices located near you.

Professionals and Specialists: Check journals published by professional associations such as *Chronicle of Higher Education* (not-for-profit academia); *Chronicle of Philanthropy* (fund-raising); *New York Law Journal* (law); *Black Engineer* (engineering); *The Chief* (NYC government); *Journal of the American Medical Association* (medicine); *Science* (scientific research); *Variety* (entertainment); *HR Journal* and *Workforce* (human resources); *Billboard* (musicians); *Women's Wear Daily* (fashion).

Unemployed: Department of Labor Job Service (America's Job Bank www.ajb.dni.us); America Works—212 244-5627; FEGS (social service organization, 212 366-8400); Goodwill Industries—neighborhood community centers.

Disabled Individuals: VESID (Vocational Educational Services for Individuals with Disabilities—www.nysed.gov/vesid/contact.htm); ICD (International Center for the Disabled—212 585-6000); centers for rehabilitation medicine; *Careers and the DisAbled* magazine.

Seniors: Career Encores—(800) 833-6267; Second Careers—www.secondcareer.com; AARP—www.aarp.org; Operation ABLE—www.ezsis.org/able/individual.html; senior citizen foundations (like www.sremploy.org); Forty Plus Club—www.socal.com/40plus.

employment agencies

Need a job fast?

Open the want ads and you'll see lots of employment agencies promoting their services. Some are geared to particular positions (secretaries, accountants, paralegals). Others specialize in certain industries (advertising, banking, health, law). But most represent a variety of industries and careers.

You may wonder whether agencies are worth bothering with. Here are some criteria that indicate when you can rely on them:

POSITIVE POINTS ABOUT AGENCIES

■ You will be counseled by a representative with knowledge of the current marketplace. In other words, someone who's aware of which companies are hiring at the moment.

■ Agencies will test your proficiency on the computer and sometimes assess your language, data entry, typing, proofreading, or mathematical abilities. Some offer remedial classes in the latest office software.

■ Agencies can usually line you up with interviews within the week and will give you tips on how to dress and present yourself. They may even touch up your resumé for you.

■ With agency representation, you don't have to wait for your resumé to be plucked from the pile, for the phone to ring, for the postcard asking you to come in for an interview. They will get your foot in the door and are a great help if you're feeling unfocused and are lacking confidence.

CONSIDERATIONS

Remember, there are some drawbacks to working with an employment agency during your job search. They have their own interests, which may not always coincide with yours. But you can benefit from working with an agency if you can make their interests work for you. Still, agencies should always be just an adjunct to your other job search efforts. Keep these points in mind when agencies send you for interviews.

NEGATIVE POINTS ABOUT AGENCIES

■ Agencies can have a square pegs into round holes mentality. They may try to hammer on you until you fit into a certain position or break into a million splinters!

■ They generally send you only to larger companies. A smaller company might have a very good job opening but can't afford to pay their fees.

■ You're not the agency's customer—the employer is. Filling the employer's job with a live person pays the rent for their beautiful office; helping you discover your life's work does not. They don't usually have a great deal of time, patience, or imagination to consider your priorities.

headhunters

The custom employment agencies

Consider the executive recruiter, or headhunter.
They are highly attuned to the marketplace and exceptionally skilled in matching the right person to the right job. Unlike the broadbrush approach of regular employment agencies, executive recruiters are very selective in presenting candidates. They deal exclusively with jobs at the upper levels of the corporate structure (and they are paid very well by the employer for such placements, usually 10 to 30 percent of the candidate's first-year salary).

But there are drawbacks: headhunters will not bother with you unless you are at the top of your game and have unusual, highly sought-after skills. Headhunters also are limited by the relatively small number of job openings that come to them. They typically approach candidates that interest them, rather than the other way around. The odds of a resumé coming in over the transom and fitting the bill are small. For this reason they seldom place a job ad, and when they do, it is usually found in a journal aimed at high-level professionals.

But headhunters do fill jobs. Professional associations generally maintain a list of headhunters who specialize in placing people within their field. If you are doing well in your career, it's prudent to make contact with several headhunters, in case they might at some point be looking for an individual with your special abilities. Just keep in mind that headhunters are more likely to help with your long-term career development than with any short-term job search.

TEMP AGENCIES

While you look for a permanent job, you might consider working in a temporary situation as a financial stopgap. "Temp" agencies are employment agencies that specialize in finding short-term help for companies—anywhere from a few days to a year. Temping is a good device for gaining experience, especially for young people who have not worked much in an office. And by temping, you could possibly gain valuable information about a field you want to know more about. And companies often do hire temps permanently.

Temp agencies once placed only clerical workers, but now some of them handle higher-level job categories, such as lawyers, recruiters, accountants, and marketing professionals. Their ads usually appear in newspapers and professional journals.

FIRST PERSON   SUCCESS STORY

Keeping my eyes open

A friend of mine took a job temping as an administrative assistant in the sales department of a major magazine. The sales staff liked her so much that they hired her as a sales trainee. Within a year she was a full-fledged salesperson.

I decided to try the same thing. I landed a similar job at another publication with no trouble. Following my friend's suggestions, I kept my eyes and ears open, observing everything the sales staff did, trying to learn how the business works.

Well, I hated it. The pressure those people endured to continually contact prospective clients really turned me off. Within a month I had decided I liked the creative department better, and I took some writing courses in night school. Now I'm turning out copy for the ads those sales departments are working so hard to get.

Larry S., Chicago, Illinois

research

Learn as much as you can before contacting a firm for an interview

You're doing great. You have your resumé in shape and you've checked out the standard sources for jobs. Now it's time to expand your knowledge about companies who have advertised job vacancies. But even more important, you can check out companies you would like to work for and find out how they hire.

Start by scanning the local business sections and reading the industry reports. See who's advertising, who's promoting, who's acquiring what. What piques your interest? Where in your chosen field do you belong? To learn more, request annual reports and other pertinent literature directly from various companies. Look up their Web sites on the Internet.

Once you've narrowed down your search to one or two companies, try to form a profile of their corporate cultures. Every company has its own way of dressing, speaking, acting; of dealing with customers, vendors and staff; of doing business.

If possible, get a handle on company history; find out what it took to build the company up to this point and where it may be headed in the future. Try to determine if your sympathies lie in the same direction—do you respect what the company stands for, the product or service it provides?

Once you've targeted a company and know something about it, focus on what you could do for them. Study different job titles and find out what specific duties are assigned to each. Consult with agencies to learn more about what is expected in those jobs. Go over the ads in newspapers and trade journals and read a description of the job at your local library in the *Dictionary of Occupational Titles* (28,000 job titles). Check salary surveys and see if they match your needs and expectations.

WHAT'S OUT THERE

Online Research: For obtaining current information about companies, an invaluable source is the Internet site for an organization called Hoovers Online, The Business Network (www.hoovers.com). For checking salary information, try www.jobsmart.org.

Association Research: Join a professional organization that serves the industry you're interested in. If possible, look for one that specializes in the area of the business you hope to become part of. At the organization's meetings you may even have the opportunity to get to know people working at companies that interest you. Through your contacts with them, you can find out about hiring practices—where they advertise and the name of the person who supervises the position that interests you.

On-the-Job Research: If you have little experience in the industry that you've targeted for yourself, consider getting a volunteer assignment or a paid or unpaid internship. No book, report, or Web site can match the vividness of personal experience. See page 73 for suggestions about how to find companies and not-for-profit groups in need of volunteers or that offer minimal-pay jobs. The real payoff comes first when you learn about the industry and second when you can put this new experience on your resumé.

See page 73 for suggestions about how to find companies

CAN'T READ AN ANNUAL REPORT?

Your best bet is to ask a friend in management or finance to show you how to interpret the figures and foresee the future viability of the company. If you aren't acquainted with such people, look at the "Guide to Understanding Financials" on the Web site for the Public Register Annual Report Service at www.prars.com.

keeping on track

Record every move during your job search so you don't lose your way

It is essential that you keep a paper trail of what you are doing during your job hunt—the more extensive the better. Start the very first day. Buy an inexpensive loose-leaf notebook. In this notebook you can maintain records throughout your job search; this is essential for helping you to recall whom you have talked to and what you talked about. Even though it may seem simplistic in the beginning, in the end, you will be very glad you did it.

■ Clip each ad (or print a copy of on-line ads) and paste it onto a page in the notebook, along with a copy of the version of your resumé and cover letter you sent in response. Sometimes it takes weeks for companies to contact you, and you may have forgotten exactly which job was in question. You'll want to reread information about the job in the language the company used to describe it.

NYC based constr co seeking qualified Accnts with job costing, A/R, A/P exp. Fax resume: Rheiner 212/659-8460 EOE.

✔ Daily Press, 1/2/01, business section
✔ Faxed Resume and Cover letter to "Attn.: Rheiner" 1/3/01
✔ Rheiner's secretary called 1/14/01 to make appt. with him 1/17/01. 10:00 a.m., at 5711 Seventh Avenue, Room 2100.
✔ Met with Larry Rheiner 1/17/01 (secretary Judy). He said that the position would be supervised by the financial VP.
✔ Office looked shabby, but Rheiner said they were moving to a new building in June. Salary would be $45,000 plus profit-sharing at year's end. I said that was slightly less than I was looking for, but if there is a year-end salary review, I would be interested.

■ Next to each ad, note the actions that result and the dates: Phone callback, Interview(s), Job Offer, Job Accepted or Declined, to help you keep track of your status at each firm.

■ Immediately after each interview, make some notes on the page while the details are still fresh in your mind. (That's what the person who interviewed you is doing.) Attach a copy of the thank-you letter you sent. If you have another interview later, you will be able to remind yourself of the impressions you had from the meeting before and prepare questions that have occurred to you.

■ Keep a list of the names and titles of people you meet at the firm other than the interviewer—a secretary, a boss who poked her head into a meeting, a possible colleague you may have met. These may come in handy later in the interviewing process.

✔ Sent thank-you note to Rheiner 1/18/01 (attached)

✔ 1/21/01 Judy called to set appt. with Financial VP George Lewis for 1/24/01 at 4:30 p.m. Camden Bank in Long Island City, 112-45 17th Avenue, Room 22-7 (he's working for two weeks on a special project in a client's office)

✔ 1/24/01 Financial VP sec called to delay appt until 1/28/01, same time and place.

✔ 1/28/01 Met with Lewis. Very nice guy, also likes the Mets and skis at Wyndom. He said the job would eventually require costing related project in Spain, and asked if I could speak Spanish. I said only French. He was interested in my work on the Gregory building. I promised to send a copy of the annual report entry on it.

✔ Sent thank-you note to Lewis 1/29/01 (attached) with annual report entry

✔ 2/1/01 Lewis called to offer me the job. I said I had a $50,000 offer from Greenbriar, but I liked Gimes better, but he wouldn't match the salary. Sent thank-you note anyway, saying I hoped to see him at the USAA convention in May.

now what do I do?

Answers to common problems

Is it worthwhile for me to join a membership association and pay dues even before I am ready to graduate and look for a job?

Yes, if the dues seem reasonable. Doing so will introduce you to the industry, giving you a chance to familiarize yourself with the jargon, current research and theories, and the "stars" who are making headlines in your proposed field of work. You can also keep an eye on the ads in their publications, using them to learn about the specific duties for different positions in that field.

What about responding to an announcement on the radio or television?

Sure. Some local firms choose this form of advertisement. The same advice applies to responses to all forms of advertising.

One big agency has been sending me around to jobs that are the opposite of what I told them I'm looking for. I don't get it. What should I do?

Pick another agency. They obviously are not listening to you, or they are discounting what you have told them. It may be that you need to try your objectives out on another agency or two and see what they say. If others have a similar reaction, consider whether your objectives may be unrealistic (such as, "I want to be a manager even though I have no experience supervising others"), or whether they may be met best by going job hunting solo (without agency intervention), in the hopes of getting a company to create the kind of job you have in mind.

Should I just take a job at my uncle's firm, as he wants me to?

You might consider it. There's no shame in getting a head start from a relative or acquaintance; it can be a sound way to gain entry into the business world. But you need to determine: 1) Do you like the industry? 2) Will the job enable you to learn and grow? 3)Will politics in the workplace make the position uncomfortable for you?

Should I do any advertising of myself as a job-seeker, as in "Positions Wanted?"

You probably won't have much luck advertising in a large newspaper, but you might catch the attention of an executive if you place an ad in a business publication or the journal of a professional association.

Would having my own Web site be a good way for me to advertise my availability?

It isn't a priority unless you are in the computer business; most recruiters don't make a habit of visiting strange Web sites. If you hope to get into the computer business, it probably would be advantageous if you could construct a professional, interesting Web site for yourself and include the address for it on your resume. But be sure it's technically bug-free, perfectly proofread, and the very ultimate in user-friendliness, or it won't be very effective advertising for you.

HELPFUL RESOURCES

WEB ADDRESSES	PUBLICATIONS
www.jobfindersonline.com	**Job Finder's Guide** by Les Krantz (note unique listing of telephone job hotlines)
Career Directions www.careers.org	
Working at Home www.aarp.org/working_options/home.html/	**CareerXroads** by Gerry Crispin and Mark Mehler
Employment Ads www.careerpath.com www.monster.com www.jobsonline.com www.recruiterresources.com	**Career Exploration on the Internet** by Laura R. Gabler

Networking

Getting the word out 70
People help you only if they know you need it

Professional meetings 72
Collecting business cards and contacts

Informational interviews 74
The insider view of the job you want

Finding a mentor 76
The ultimate in networking

Cold calls 78
Talking to complete strangers

Now what do I do? 80
Answers to common problems

Gallery openings, dinners at friends' homes, chance meetings while traveling—all are opportunities to exchange business cards and gather information.

getting the word out

Someone you barely know may get you your next job

Picture this: You're new to town. You need a hairdresser, dry cleaners, foot doctor. What do you do? You ask your neighbors, family, friends, coworkers, minister, rabbi for referrals. Soon suggestions and referrals come rolling in. This is Basic Networking 101. It functions pretty much the same whether you're looking for a good hairdresser or a good job.

It is essential that you get the word out that you are job hunting. And the message has to be spread wide because research shows it's unlikely that anyone in your inner circle will provide the crucial piece to the job puzzle. Rather, someone on the periphery of your contacts will end up giving you the tip that matters—the newsstand guy's daughter, for example.

Why do casual acquaintances want to help? Call it human nature. Most people like to be able to do favors when they can. And a referral is so easy to do.

SK THE EXPERTS

I'm going to a party. A guy who works at a company I want to work for will be there as well. Should I approach him?

Yes. Introduce yourself, say you're interested in working at his company. Then ask about his job and what he thinks of the organization. Show your interest in him and his situation before you get back to yourself.

Should I ask this person, or any friend for that matter, to make calls for me to find out about job openings?

Yes, but don't presume on people's time. Ask only for favors that can be done in a few minutes. If you want your contact to spend an hour making calls for you, it's just not going to happen, and you'll alienate that person by asking. And don't be demanding. You may want a friend to make a call for you, but you must wait until he finds it convenient.

How do I show my gratitude to someone who helps me?

Express your thanks. Write or call to show your appreciation for every effort—even when a tip doesn't pan out. And once you've got a job, don't drop people who tried to help you; apprise everyone in your network of your progress after a few months or a year. Finally, always return favors, if you can, at some future date. An interactive network, ever-expanding, should be built to last through a long and prosperous career.

TO PRESS OR NOT TO PRESS

Take care that you keep your networking efforts friendly. You may be aching for a job, but you must show people that you are interested in their affairs as well as yours. If you constantly talk only about your own needs, you will soon earn an unpleasant reputation as a self-seeking user, rather than a person who wants to interact and make friends, and everyone will steer clear of you.

professional meetings

All those business cards you collected may help you land your next job

A prime place for trading job information is at the "professional meeting." Conventions within the industry are one example. Another is a meeting of any professional association connected to the industry. At almost every one of these gatherings there is considerable exchange about job openings and opportunities, information about a job club that meets separately, or a newsletter featuring job leads.

Not only should you attend professional meetings in the field in which you want to find a job, you should take it a step further and volunteer for a committee or assist in setting up a meeting. If you already have experience in the profession, see if you can arrange to be a guest speaker at the next convention or write an article for the association newsletter.

Once you get to the meeting, don't hang back. Talk to, and exchange cards with, as many people as you can. If you have expertise in a particular subject—speak up! After the meeting, send a note to people you've met. Try to set up lunch dates or other meetings to help you stay in touch with people who are knowledgeable in your field.

Back home, don't forget to visit the association's Web site, chat rooms, and listserve (an e-mail service that forwards your message to the whole membership or a group within it). Become an active, recognized participant. These are great ways to increase your visibility and show people what you're all about. Then when they see your name on a resumé, it will already have a familiar ring to it.

Professional meetings may also provide you with something else invaluable to your success—a mentor. Look at page 76 for more information on this subject.

NETWORKING OPPORTUNITIES

Many successful business people make contacts outside work that help them progress in their designated careers:

SPORTS: "Women need to learn to play golf," says an assistant treasurer and branch manager of Chase. "That's where the business deals are cut!" But other types of sporting activities work just as well. Diana P. heard of a high-level job opening in her company at her son's Little League game while seated on the bleachers next to the president of the firm.

THE CHARITY CIRCUIT: Many corporations advocate community involvement for their employees as beneficial for the company profile. It also enhances your own image and builds your network as you meet other professionals who volunteer. For ideas about volunteer organizations, look on the Internet at www.volunteermatch.org (search by your zipcode) or www.give.org.

THE CLASSROOM: Furthering your education can bring you into contact with executives in other firms while it enhances your job skills. Many people participating in an Executive MBA program (an advanced degree in business), for example, have made connections that have proved beneficial to their careers.

THE SOCIAL EVENT: Gallery openings, dinners at friends' homes, chance meetings while traveling—all are opportunities to exchange business cards and gather information.

informational interviews

A friendly chat can advance your career search

How did you get your job?

Your next step is to request an informational interview at companies that interest you. Find the name of a person who is doing the job you want to do, either through professional meetings or other contacts. Ask for no more than 20 minutes in person to discuss the field and promise not to ask for a job. Always keep your promise or your credibility will be tarnished. Ask questions, create a positive impression, see the job environment firsthand, and obtain specific information. At the end, ask your interviewee for two additional contacts.

Before long, if you send out appropriate thank-you's, keep in touch with all your contacts, and meet for lunch occasionally, you will have built a professional network—from scratch. You also will have learned about several particular companies from people in the know.

As your search progresses, you should be able to determine who in the company that interests you has the hiring authority for the position you seek. Comb your network for a person or persons who know that head honcho, and get them to introduce you, or allow you to use their names as reference. Then write or call for an interview with this person. Although there may be no specific position open, you can make points by showing that you are interested in the company and asking good questions about the job you're hoping for.

Questions to Ask on an Informational Interview

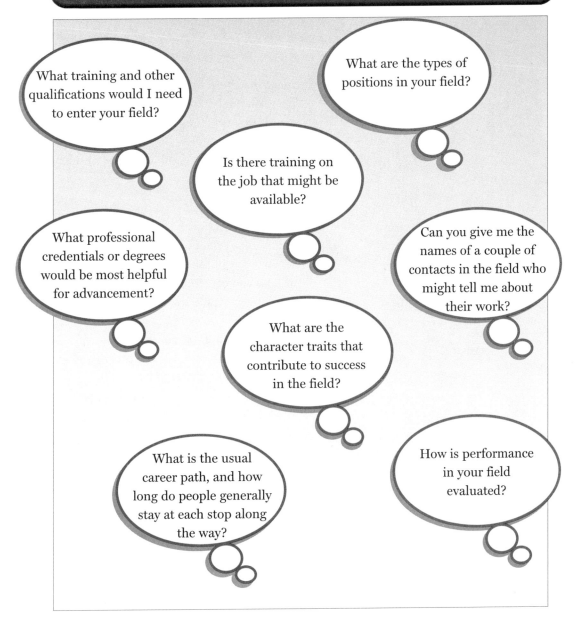

What training and other qualifications would I need to enter your field?

What are the types of positions in your field?

Is there training on the job that might be available?

What professional credentials or degrees would be most helpful for advancement?

Can you give me the names of a couple of contacts in the field who might tell me about their work?

What are the character traits that contribute to success in the field?

What is the usual career path, and how long do people generally stay at each stop along the way?

How is performance in your field evaluated?

finding a mentor

The ultimate networking coup— connecting with a guru

If you can persuade a more experienced and seasoned professional to take an interest in you personally, you will be that much more likely to succeed in your chosen career. Such a guide can steer you away from common pitfalls, teach you how to play the corporate game, and point out different paths to the top. Worth looking for!

Ideally, you want a mentor to help you for many years, so take some care in finding a good one. Look at people in the corporate levels above you in your firm or others in the same business. Decide which of them you most admire. Consider personal integrity, problem-solving abilities and people skills, as well as talents specifically related to the field you're in.

Then find a way to tell that person in a note— or in person, if the opportunity presents itself—about the qualities you admire most in him or her, and ask for a bit of specific advice about how you can emulate those winning ways. Even the busiest people will usually take the time to talk to you about themselves for a few minutes. "You'd be surprised at how rarely I say no to young people who want help or advice," Linda Srere, chief operating officer at Young & Rubicam (a large advertising and marketing firm), said to a *Fortune* interviewer. "People at my level understand the importance of doing this."

When you report back how you put the advice to good use, you have opened the path for another bit of advice. Little by little, over months and years, your relationship with your mentor will grow.

As your mentor shares experiences, critiques and supports your decisions, and offers personal guidance through the corporate maze, your capabilities will grow, and your career is likely to be enhanced. Through the years, you may find more than one mentor to help you, some of them perhaps outside your industry or profession. All the better.

ASK THE EXPERTS

My boss is really kind and gives me good advice. Does that make him my mentor?

No, not always. You may learn a great deal from a boss, but he may not help you move forward in your career because you could be more valuable to him staying where you are. It is usually better to look for a mentor who is several levels above you, or in another department, or even in another firm.

There are two very senior people in my office who would be ideal mentors. Both seem willing to help me. How do I decide between them?

Consider personality fit, age, and the amount of time each one is likely to have to give. If both are similar, ask each one for advice on the same problem and compare the answers. Choose the one whose answer seems more farsighted. But do make a decision between them. Otherwise, you may find yourself with divided loyalties and caught in the crossfire of corporate politics from time to time. That doesn't mean you shouldn't be friendly with the one you did not choose. You just shouldn't try to juggle two very close relationships.

cold calls

Sometimes you may have to dig up your own contacts

Occasionally the network fails you. Despite your best efforts, you may not be able to find a contact for a company that interests you. That is when the cold call becomes necessary.

A cold call is just that—calling someone you don't know and asking for something. You'd be too nervous? Don't worry, there's a trick to staying cool. Start by developing a script. Then, when you have a contact on the phone, you can follow this script, and you'll sound perfectly calm.

As you write your script, think in terms of asking for information (see page 75). You will want to develop a couple of specific questions about the nature of the department in which you want to work. Then add a two-sentence summary of your most important qualifications. Remember, you want to say how your qualifications could benefit this person, or this company. Never, never ask how they could benefit you.

With your preparation in hand, speak to the receptionist at your ideal company and ask to be transferred to the person in charge of hiring for the area you want to work in. Time your call for the end of the day or right before lunch—most executives pick up their own phones at those times, and you won't have to run interference with their assistants or secretaries.

Introduce yourself and explain (quickly) that you are interested in working for the company. Lay it on the line in your best sales manner—a two-sentence summary of your most important qualifications. Run through your short list of questions about the nature of the work in her area, and tell her your qualifications. If you're polite and professional, at the very least the person at the other end will be receptive to you.

Then ask for an appointment for an informational interview.

IF THE ANSWER IS "WE'RE NOT HIRING"

Think about the worst thing that can happen after you go through your script. The person might say there are no openings at present. That's the worst. She can't bite you. So how do you answer her if that is indeed what you hear?

Tell her you would appreciate finding out how you might fit in at some future point. Ask for an informational interview sometime during the next few weeks.

If she says it isn't convenient to meet, ask if she can recommend any other person in the company who might be able to tell you more about the area that interests you.

Then send her a thank-you letter that includes a short summary of your skills—just in case something occurs to her later.

FIRST PERSON **SUCCESS STORY**

Reaching into the unknown

The benefits of networking can turn up the most unexpected opportunities. I was writing freelance for several trade journals, but had longed to get into a big-time publication. Reluctantly, at my husband's urging, I called my sister-in-law's sister's new boyfriend, an editor at a large metropolitan daily newspaper. I had never even met him. He was not too encouraging, but he gave me the name of one of the editors at the paper who he thought might be interested in the type of articles I wanted to do. That editor passed my resumé and cover letter on to another, along with copies of two stories I had written. Within a few weeks I got my first writing assignment for them, and a month after that I was put on staff.

Melodie K., Columbus, Ohio

now what do I do?

Answers to common problems

How can I find out about internships in my area?

A good place to start is with college placement offices, local businesses, nonprofit organizations, charities, schools, athletic organizations, and hospitals. The Internet can be a useful resource too. Use any search engine such as Yahoo! or Excite for "Volunteer AND Opportunities," and you'll get a slew of Web sites guiding you to internships all over the country. To name a few: www.4work.com links you with the location you want and the type of internship (marketing intern in NYC); www.idealist.org has access to 20,000 organizations in 140 countries and will match you with internships in non-profit organizations; www.councilexchanges.org will tell you about volunteering around the world. The good old-fashioned telephone can yield information too, for example: 1-800-VOLUNTEER for Point of Light Foundation; 1-888-77YOUTH for National 4-H Club; 1-888-559-6884 for National Mentoring Partnership.

I'm too shy to network. Do I have to?

No, networking is not for everyone. But it can be learned. Try practicing with those close to you and then someone who's just an acquaintance. Ask them to give you a gentle critique. Listen to the feedback—are you too laid-back, too pushy, too soft-spoken? You'll find as you do it you'll get more confident. Try to think about it as a two-way street. The person who gives you a lead may be the same person you can help in the future, once you're in your new position.

I want to make a switch from nursing. I've taken some courses in accounting. How can I tell if I'd really like being an accountant?

An internship of six months would be ideal for you. It would give you hands-on experience in your new chosen field. You'd see if you truly like the day-to-day routine of an accounting department and what role you would like to pursue, short term and long term. If this is not financially feasible, find a way to get this same experience by volunteering at your church or perhaps for a local charity group. Non-profit organizations always need help with their books!

How do I know if my mentor is giving me good advice?

Look at your mentor's career, her allegiances within her company, her general philosophy about life and work. Does it match your own? Is it admirable? Check out some of her advice with a third party—is it off the wall or fairly standard? In the final analysis, you are your own person and will have to make your own decisions in your work life (as you do in your personal life). Always take any advice with a little grain of salt.

 ## HELPFUL RESOURCES

WEB ADDRESSES	PUBLICATIONS
www.careermag.com www.monster.com	**Mentorship: The Essential Guide for School and Business** by Jill M. Reilly

Interviews

The process. 84
Who are you going to meet?

In the waiting room. 86
Pre-interview behavior counts too

Trade secrets. 88
How to psyche out your interviewer

The tangibles. 90
Putting your experience on the table

Subjects to avoid. 92
Practice your diplomatic skills

The intangibles. 94
Interpersonal skills make the difference

The tough questions. 96
Avoid panic by planning your answers

After the interview. 98
Follow up for a lasting impression

Sample thank-you letters. 100
Reiterate what happened in the interview

A second interview. 102
A callback narrows the competition

Now what do I do?!. 104
Answers to common problems

An interviewer must decide if the company
can get a good return by investing in you.

the process

The drill can vary, depending on the size of the company and the type of business

Terrific, you landed an interview. But who are you going to see? Well, that depends on the company. Most businesses are small, 50 employees or less. In companies of that size, you are likely to meet with the top person, who probably owns the company as well. While you wait for your appointment, a receptionist may ask you to fill out a simple application form.

At a big organization, the scenario can vary. If your interview has been made because you answered an ad, chances are that ad was developed by the personnel department, also known as the human resources department. Your first stop will probably be a screening interview with someone in that department—a person called an interviewer or recruiter. If you make it past that person, you will be eligible for another interview, this time most likely with your potential boss. Chances are there will be only two or three candidates still in the running at this point, since the others will have been winnowed out by the screening interviews.

If your interview at a large firm results from a personal contact you have made with your potential boss, you might be interviewed by him first. Then, when he is ready to hire you, he could either see you again personally or he could route you back to the human resources people, who would check your background and brief you about benefits.

At any stage of the game, be prepared for more than one interview. There may be layers in the company hierarchy, and people in each of these layers may want to have some input in the hiring process. And as the field of candidates narrows, the interviews become more extensive and detailed.

ASK THE EXPERTS

I get anxious about competition. How should I act if I happen to meet someone else who's interviewing for the same job?

Make friends. Yes, you heard right. You never know when and where you will come in contact with that person again. Maybe the company will hire both of you, and you will be working together. Maybe he will be hired and then promoted; later, he could end up hiring you. Or he may land at another great company, and remember you when they need a new employee. Each industry is a relatively small community. Every contact you make could be valuable at some time or another. You'll lose that option if you act hostile and make an unnecessary enemy, even if you're eager for the job.

What can I do if a human resources interviewer screens me out before I meet a potential boss?

Look for a networking contact, within the company or through personal or professional channels, who can tell you who the prospective boss is. Then make a cold call to her, describing your credentials (see Cold Calls, page 78-79). She's ready to hire someone; perhaps your presentation of yourself will be more effective with her than with the HR department.

Are there subjects that my former employer cannot bring up when asked about my previous work?

Lawsuits have made former employers jumpy about giving out too much information for fear of being accused of defamation, invasion of privacy, or emotional distress. They usually give your title and dates of employment, and confirm your salary if the caller mentions a specific figure. Most former employers also require a written request for a reference signed by you. In cases of misconduct, however, former employers may "in good faith" divulge more if they stick carefully to the facts.

Companies are likely to ask you for a list of references, and they no doubt will contact some of them. In fact, if a hiring company does not attempt to check your references, it can be sued for "negligent hiring."

Be sure to contact friends and former employers to get their permission before you name them as references. Ask them if they can speak positively about your professional contributions and personal attributes.

Generally, interviewers frown on typed letters of reference and prefer to speak directly with the person giving the reference. In that way, they can ask questions pertinent to their concerns.

in the waiting room

Don't sabotage yourself before you even meet the interviewer

There you are, waiting to have your interview. Perhaps it's a preliminary interview with human resources, or maybe it's a second interview with someone who could be your new boss. Either way, the anxiety level is creeping up.

Sure you're nervous. The problem is, that anxiety may show itself in unfortunate ways. Sometimes it can end your job hunt before you even meet anyone who might want to hire you.

A case of nerves need not be debilitating. Many professional speakers, athletes, musicians, and actors suffer agonizing pre-performance jitters, but they use them to energize themselves. However, if you are not experienced in transforming your anxiety into positive action, it can cause you to behave in an uncharacteristically foolish manner.

Unfortunately, interviewers are likely to hear about almost everything that goes on in the waiting room. So be careful what you do and say.

DOS AND DON'TS FOR APPLICATION FORMS

Make it easy on yourself and fill them out carefully

DO
- Print legibly—and watch your spelling too!
- Put down a real reason for leaving a job. Supply the necessary information for background checking (credit, criminal record, employment history) and for voluntary EEOC ethnic identification.
- Sign and date the form.

DON'T
- Write "please see resumé." The company needs you to sign off on the accuracy of the information you put down on the application, so supply details on their form.
- Veer off into any fiction, such as passing off a friend as your supervisor. Everything is subject to fact and reference checking. A lie —or even an exaggeration—might cost you the job.
- Argue about filling out the forms—ever. This is an opportunity to show you are a team player and will abide by the company's policies and procedures.

PRE-GAME PARAMETERS

Don't fidget. When one interviewer went home with a migraine, another was forced to take on the extra workload. This meant that all the candidates were kept waiting, although no explanation was given to them. After sitting for 20 minutes, one applicant began pacing about the lobby, scowling and glowering at nearby employees. Round and round he went. When the interviewer heard about the applicant's behavior, needless to say, she gave him a short interview.

Respect the rules. When a candidate for a senior position refused to complete an employment application, an administrative assistant met with him to explain the legal reasons such forms are required. The applicant impatiently grabbed the application and sat down, slamming his briefcase into nearby furniture. He returned the application partially completed. He forgot that companies prefer team players to bullies, and a show of respect to a display of anarchy. He never got to round two.

Be professional. A recent college graduate became confrontational when asked to take a typing test. "My mother didn't put me through college so I could be a typist!" she told the hapless receptionist. "Should I write on your application that you refused to take the test?" the receptionist inquired. Reluctantly, the grad took the test (after the computer was turned on for her). It was too late, though. Her protestations made everyone leery about her ability to deal with vendors, customers, and staff.

Mind your manners. A candidate showed her disdain for human resources personnel with rude, pointed behavior. "Have a seat over there, and you can read the company literature while you wait," induced elaborate eye-rolling. When told the interviewer would be with her in a moment, she glared repeatedly at her watch. Her rude behavior was reported to her prospective interviewer. Another short interview. She didn't seem to know that manners are paramount in the business world.

trade secrets

Psyching out your interviewer can help land the job

Yes, you've prepared for the interview. You've read up on the company. You've given some thought to how you can put the best possible face on your past professional life. You have practiced expounding confidently on your ability to take on bigger and better projects in the future. But have you stopped to consider the person sitting opposite you?

Perhaps you've heard that interviewers (both the human resources variety and prospective bosses) tend to hire people who are like them. Well, that's not exactly true. But there are some secrets to the interviewing process you might want to consider:

TRADE SECRET ONE

Interviewers hire people with whom they feel comfortable. If you make the interviewer uncomfortable, you don't stand a chance. Any human resources interviewer can tell you about his negative reaction to candidates ushered into his office who are certain they have the job and act annoyed at having to go through HR. The interviewer then has to question whether they can handle petty annoyances that are part of every job in the real world. Such candidates could end up losing their chances for employment.

TRADE SECRET TWO

The unknown frightens interviewers. If you clam up and respond entirely in monosyllables, the interviewer will have to drag information out of you and make guesses about what you are hiding, which will make him very unhappy. He needs to be reasonably confident that he understands what you are like.

TRADE SECRET THREE

The way you behave is of paramount importance. If you use slang and colloquialisms, are overly familiar with the interviewer, or disrespectful, rude, uncooperative, or resistant, the interviewer will question how you'd interact with clients, vendors, and coworkers. Could he count on you to be appropriate and professional?

INTERVIEW ETIQUETTE

Start out on the right foot by being friendly, forthcoming, and businesslike in your responses. You are more likely to convey the impression that you are easy to be around and enthusiastic about the possibilities of working for the company.

Look neat. Wear a hairstyle and business clothing that are fashionable, but not elaborate or showy.

Be polite. Shake hands. Say thank you for little things, such as the cup of coffee you are offered or help you're given with your coat. Don't sit down until the interviewer does. If you are introduced to someone else who enters the room, stand up and offer your hand.

Be responsive. Maintain normal eye contact during conversations. Establish a give-and-take conversation, but without constantly interrupting the interviewer or monopolizing the conversation.

Ask questions. Indicate that you are interested in the product or services offered by the company, and that you are eager and willing to do the job.

Be helpful. Do what you can to assist the interviewer in assessing whether you are a good match for the job. Talk about how your background suits you for the position that has been described, not about your current hobbies.

the tangibles

They're what you have to put on the table

Once an interviewer's comfort level is assured, she proceeds to evaluate how right you are for the job in question. She looks first for the basics—education, experience, and skills.

A potential boss or HR interviewer will want to gauge how you (an unknown) will function on a new job. To do that, both will try to

predict the future from your past performance and your present circumstances. So recount your successes and your accomplishments. Lightly touch on your failures (and what you learned from them). Explain your goals and the steps you've taken to reach them. Stress your ability to juggle multiple responsibilities. Show that you are reasonably articulate, confident, and intelligent. And don't be afraid to display some humor.

Let the interviewer know about all the specific skills you bring to the workplace so she can judge whether they match the job she has. She also may want to find out if you're interested in improving your current skills, which may mean putting in extra time and effort. Tell her that you are. (If you're not, this may be the wrong job for you.)

If you are inexperienced or have been working on your own, she may wonder if you've ever been part of an office team or if the office routine and hierarchy will come as a shock to you. Reassure her that you know what's expected. (Then if you don't, ask an experienced friend to brief you later.)

SK THE EXPERTS

What's the proper way to ask an interviewer to clarify the job description?

One job seeker complained to the human resources director that the people who had interviewed him at the company seemed confused about the nature of the available job. He was right to try to get more accurate information about the job, but his accusatory, get-your-act-together tone alienated the very people who might influence his hire. He should have asked politely—again and again if necessary—if a written job description was available. If not, he should have taken notes, then reviewed them with his prospective boss, beginning with, "As I understand it, this position requires ... "

How much should I talk?

When interviewers ask open-ended questions, they are hoping you will expand a little on the topic. However, you must be wary of motor-mouth syndrome. Do not attempt to take control of the interview away from the interviewer. If you engage in a monologue, you will prevent him from exploring other topics with you. Just answer the question, giving specific examples to back up your statements, then look to your interviewer for cues on whether to continue or wait for the next topic.

Is it all right to ask about company benefits?

You should not ask about benefits during the interview process. The interviewer wants to know what you can do for him, not vice versa. Instead, be prepared to ask about the company's latest acquisitions, the mergers, the new product line, the five-year plan. You want to prove that you've done your research and have some understanding of the company and its place in the industry. Save the benefits questions until after you've been offered the job. At that point, if you are not happy with them, you may be able to negotiate for more.

subjects to avoid

Tread carefully around touchy matters

Talking about trouble in your past work history can be dicey. If you detail the failings of another company and its associates, your strategy can backfire. After all, the interviewer doesn't know you well enough to judge where the problem originated. All she hears is that there were problems. She may think there could be more problems if she hires you.

A good rule of thumb is to put a positive light on everything that's happened to you previously. If your former boss was a Neanderthal, state simply that you had a "difference in management philosophies," but you admired his "strong convictions." If you were fired, don't blame others. Explain simply that any trouble you had has taught you a difficult lesson, and now you will be able to use it to your advantage in building a stronger career. Period. Don't dwell on the problem. But if you can put it in context—"A third of Mr. Johnson's staff has left this year,"—say that as well. Whatever the past difficulties are that might come up, rehearse what you will say about them beforehand.

FIRST PERSON DISASTER STORY

Ahead of myself

After I'd spent months looking for work, a friend called to say there was an opening at her company. She gave my resumé to the human resources people. When I met with them, I told them how great I'd be in the job—I knew all the latest accounting changes, and I could manage anybody. I'd been doing that at all my interviews, trying to exude confidence. But this job I really knew I could do. I asked them about benefits. They were very nice, and I was sure I was in. Then nothing. No calls, nothing. My friend finally told me they had chosen someone else. I was crushed. What happened? The human resources manager had told my friend I was the most arrogant candidate they had ever interviewed, and my questions about benefits were way too premature. My friend said I may have been overconfident, but she was sure I'd do fine the next time. And sure enough, I did tone it down on my next interview, and I got that job.

Cindy M., Montgomery, Alabama

SUBJECTS INTERVIEWERS CAN'T BRING UP

Whether you are being interviewed by an agency, a headhunter, human resources people, or prospective bosses, it is illegal for any of them to ask you about the following:

■ Your race, color, religion or creed, sex, or national origin (according to Title VII of the Federal Civil Rights Act of 1964).

■ Your age, especially if you are 40 or older (according to the Age Discrimination in Employment Act, 1967).

■ Your arrest record. However, you can be asked about any convictions.

■ Any disability you have. However, you do have to answer the following: "These are the requirements of the job; is there anything that would prevent you from performing the essential duties of this job? If yes, what type of accommodation would allow you to perform these duties?"

In certain states questions about your marital status, sexual orientation, and veteran status are also prohibited; find out what the law is in your state by calling the state's Department of Labor or checking its Web site.

the intangibles

Those all-important interpersonal skills

While an interviewer is asking about your background, education, likes and dislikes, hobbies, and skills, he is also seeking to find out how good your interpersonal skills are. You need to reassure him, starting when you first walk into the office.

You should be friendly, engaging, and professional to every person you set eyes on, from the FedEx man (who doesn't even work for the company) to the vice president. Think Candid Camera, and don't let your guard down for a second. You can demonstrate by your demeanor, the tone of your voice, and your style of communication that you can make things easier, not harder, for everyone around you. Behaving inappropriately—being overly chummy, condescending, obsequious, or critical—can ruin an interview.

It all comes down to a pleasing personality, and that is an attribute that really counts, probably much more than you think. If personality is not your strong suit, you can dodge problems by practicing an interview with friends who promise to give you honest feedback. Ask them to tell you about your tone of voice, degree of assertiveness, observation of etiquette, and ability to interact successfully with others. You may find that up to this point you've been unknowingly shooting yourself in the foot with an unpleasant manner.

WHAT THE INTERVIEWER REALLY WANTS TO ASK YOU

The unspoken question any interviewer must answer in her own mind is, will you be a good employee? This is true to some extent for a human resources recruiter, but it is crucial for any prospective boss. To answer that question she will look first and foremost for someone who will not constantly challenge her authority and who will make her look good.

Next, an interviewer must decide if the company can get a good return by investing in you. Can she be proud to have okayed your joining the company, or will hiring you be a mistake that will reflect badly on her? After all, she can lose credibility if you turn out to be a jerk that no one can stomach.

Here's a review of some of the unspoken questions you'll want to reassure her about:

■ Will you get along with colleagues, subordinates, and superiors? Also clients? Also vendors? Is it evident that you're a team player?

■ Are you a person who respects authority and understands the corporate hierarchy? Will you understand your position and how you fit into the scheme of things?

■ Will you follow company rules or will you think policies and procedures are made to be broken? Do you believe rules are for other people?

■ Are you conscientious about your work and proud of what you produce?

■ Are you enthusiastic about improving your skills and acquiring new ones? Will the company be able to train and promote you?

the tough questions

*You can keep
your cool
if you know
what to expect*

Now that you know what's on the interviewer's mind, you can better understand how to showcase your talents in a manner that will answer his unspoken questions. But what about the tough questions he does ask? Here are some of the queries that threaten the average applicant's equilibrium:

The tell-all strategy: "Tell me about yourself." How do you avoid rambling, chewing the ear off your interviewer or shrugging off this question? Rehearse a script for yourself that highlights challenges you have encountered at work or at school. Then be quiet, and wait for the next question.

The surprise: "What's your passion?" Don't panic. The interviewer wants you to relax and let loose with some creativity. The interviewer's trying to get beyond canned answers to see what makes you tick. It's your cue to open up a little.

The strength and weakness ploy: "What was your greatest failure and what have you learned from it?" Think out in advance which failing you want to admit to and how you compensated for it. Think of a past event that you've been able to turn around. Explain how you have improved your work to avoid having a similar problem arise again. (Do the same planning for "What was your greatest accomplishment?")

The future: "What are your goals?" Indulge in some self-reflection. Name skills you want to improve, new directions you want to try. Stick to work goals, not personal ones.

The what-if: "What if an irate customer...?" Scenario questions like this one test your ability to think on your feet, exercise good judgment, and perform under pressure. Think of a few situations that might come up in your line of work, and prepare a script of ticklish situations you've handled in the past. If you really don't know what you'd do, say that you'd ask your boss for advice.

PREPARATION

Recruiters say that only about 20 to 30 percent of candidates even bother to prepare for interviews. By taking the time to consider the kinds of questions you're likely to be asked, you should fare measurably better than your competition.

A Collection of Tricky Ones

Of course, you cannot foresee every possible question that might be thrown at you, but here are some doozies that might surface in the midst of an interview. Don't let them stump you. Prepare by thinking about answers that will demonstrate that you are a problem solver, not a problem maker.

- Which work experiences have been most valuable to you and why?

- Why are you interested in our organization?

- What makes you think you can handle this position?

- How would your last supervisor describe you?

- What management skills do you have?

- What challenges are you looking for in this position?

- What type of manager do you prefer working with?

- Tell me about a difficult situation you've handled.

- What was the worst mistake in your career so far?

- Why should I hire you?

It is important to realize that the interviewer is not trying to make a fool of you with these questions. On the contrary, as your prospective boss, she hopes you'll answer brilliantly. For her, finding a good employee is like falling in love, or getting hooked on the house the real estate agent shows her or choosing the best puppy at the pound. When she sees someone whom she believes she can work with, it "feels right" to her. She'll decide you are the one if you show the potential and desire to do the work she's proposed for you, and if she intuits that the two of you will work well together.

after the interview

*How to leave
a lasting
impression*

The interview's over. You did it! You feel you made a lasting impression, and now you want to follow up. At the close of the interview, you asked about the company's timetable for hiring. You were told that they hoped to conclude interviewing and fill the position by a certain date. Now what? You don't want to be lost in a sea of resumés and applications, and have your face and your performance become a blur in the interviewer's memory.

The best follow-up is a short thank-you note to every person in the company who interviewed you—the human resources recruiter, the hiring manager, the coworkers you met. Each note should be individualized. It is most important that you relate back to specific points in the conversation that you had with each interviewer. That's one reason why those notes you made when you came away from the interview are so important (pages 64-65).

In your thank-you letters, always thank people you spoke with for their time. Tell them how much you appreciated the opportunity to meet with them and gain a greater understanding of the workings of the company. Remember, courtesy counts and will help you stand out from the crowd.

ASK THE EXPERTS

Should I call to find out whether I got the job or will be asked back for another interview?

Calling after an interview is seldom a good idea if the company is sizable. There could be a number of people who have been interviewed, and possibly the interviewer is also seeing people for other jobs. Your phone call may not be appreciated because everyone is just too busy to stop what they are doing to retrieve your resumé and other papers from the file that has been prepared for follow-through.

What if the company is small, say, fewer than 50 employees?

In a smaller company, the interviewer or prospective boss may not have seen many people for the job. Speaking by phone or e-mailing after a week might be just the thing to remind that person of your continued interest and outstanding qualities. But you are taking a risk, so if no one is interested in giving you an answer, get off the phone and don't try again.

Who follows up if an agency arranged my interview?

If you have been sent for an interview by an agency or a headhunter, they will make the follow-up calls for you. But you still need to write your thank-you letters.

sample thank-you letters

qualifications and your belief that you are well-suited for the position in question by stressing the matches between your abilities and the job description.

Karen Knight
55 Hilltop Crest
Albany, NY 10507

Knight@koolmail.com

Dear Mr. Green:

Name the position you were interviewing for, especially if the company is a large one

Thank you for taking the time to meet with me on March 3 to discuss the position of Administrative Assistant in the marketing department. The projects you described for the coming year—particularly the move to globalize operations—sound very exciting. This is exactly the kind of work I helped to facilitate at my former position at ABC Corporation.

Let me restate briefly my strengths as an Administrative Assistant for your international program:

Reiterate your strong points

• Top-notch secretarial skills including competency in Word 2000, Powerpoint, Quark, Excel, Publisher, and Access.

• Recognized ability to prioritize projects, run a well-organized desk, stay cool under pressure, and keep up with the demands of several executives.

Mention your special skills

• Fluency in Spanish from a year living in Madrid.

I appreciate hearing about your company, and look forward to speaking with you again about this opening. You can reach me at (215) 555-7250.

Sincerely yours,

Remind the interviewer of who you are and what
you talked about. Perhaps you can add some further
ideas that have occurred to you about an area touched
upon during your interview. This is especially important
if you feel that any of your answers during the interview
itself might have been less than clear.

Karen Knight   Knight@koolmail.com
55 Hilltop Crest
Albany, NY 10507

Dear Mr. Green:

I very much enjoyed meeting with you last Friday, and talking
about the future direction of Zed Corporation and how the new
human resources director will fit in. As a committed "communicator" myself, I feel sure that I could usher in a period of improved
communications among all levels of the Zed staff. As we discussed,
I previously established a formal in-house training program, such
as the one you are planning to strengthen the supervisory and
technical capabilities of your employees.

In my past two positions I've succeeded in bringing together dis-
parate elements within a company and persuading them to work as
parts of the same team. Superiors have commented that I am a col-
laborative facilitator who promotes cooperation among my colleagues across departmental lines. My contributions to special
projects and organization of company-wide events have brought
me commendations from upper-level management. I know these
attributes would be valuable to me as the human resources director at Zed.

Thank you for taking the time to brief me on your expectations for
the department. I look forward to learning more about the challenges that confront Zed from your directors at a future meeting. You
may contact me by means of my message machine, (215) 555-7250.

Sincerely yours,

Refer to matters that you discussed in your meeting

Add points that did not occur to you during the interview

Thank the individual for his time and thoroughness

Put in a number where you can be contacted, in case your resumé is mislaid

a second interview

Passed the first hurdle with honors. Now what?!

on how you feel about the company, the folks you've met so far, the type of cog you'd be in the corporate machinery. It's a little like being asked out for a second date by someone you don't know very well and whose intentions you don't entirely trust. Should you accept, and take a chance on a real match? Or, if your instincts warned you off on the first interview, should you decline politely and hope your sixth sense is reliable?

It's almost always best to go on a second interview, just to get more information. After all, if the company impressed you, you surely have more questions after an initial meeting, and this is the time to get them answered. The second meeting can be used to confirm positive points and clear up small details that have occurred to you in the interim.

If your first impression of the company was not so hot, a second meeting could be used to confirm what you feared. After all, you may have misjudged that job or the company itself. If you're asked back, use the occasion to double-check on whether or not you're passing up an opportunity that could be better than you first thought.

The good news is, someone somewhere shook your hand, sized you up, and found you absolutely satisfactory—and maybe even more. You've made it over the first hurdle. But the narrower field will be more competitive. So keep your interview performance level high.

ASK THE EXPERTS

How do I prepare for the second meeting?

Do more research and investigation by reading any company literature you've been given and spending time on the company Web site. Rehearse a scenario that suggests how your talents might contribute to the company's goals. Focus on parallels between what you've done before and what the job requires.

How do I act when I meet a person who interviewed me before? "Hi, Joe, it's good to see you again, pal!" or something less casual?

Always err on the side of formality. You needn't be stiff, but be professional. If everyone goes by first names, or you've been told to call the interviewer by his first name, then go ahead. Another tactic is to avoid names altogether and simply say, "Hello, it's good to see you again."

What if I get an offer?

This happens often. The interviewer wants a second look before deciding and sometimes he will make a choice on the spot. Be prepared to discuss compensation (see tips on negotiating in Chapter 7). But don't be shy about asking for a few days to think over a proposal. Inquire about whom to talk to in the human resources department regarding benefits. Then call back when you said you would, and give a definite answer.

How do I know where I stand?

If no offer is forthcoming, ask your interviewer what the next step is. Ask about the timetable for filling this job. Indicate that you are interested in the position and the company. Follow up with another thank-you letter summarizing points that you discussed in the second meeting.

now what do I do?

Answers to common problems

So many companies these days seem to have "dress-down" policies that I'm confused about what to wear to an interview. What do you suggest?

It's always better to err on the side of dressing up rather than down. The idea is to portray yourself as a consummate professional: crisp, clean, efficient, and orderly.

For women, wear a nice business suit or tailored dress, stockings, and low heels. Go easy on the perfume and makeup. Trim those over-long nails and skip the bright nail polish. Handbags should be small. Don't tote huge shopping bags with you. Keep jewelry low-key.

For men, wear a suit and tie, and polish your shoes. Make sure to wear an ironed shirt. Keep cologne light. Your face should be closely shaven or, if you have a beard or mustache, it should be well-trimmed.

Suppose I decide during the interview that I'm really not interested in the job?

Thank the interviewer for her time, but make it clear that you don't feel your background and your abilities match what is needed for this particular position. Don't hesitate to tell her the reason: for example, "This job involves fielding a lot of queries, and I have no experience in that type of work. If you have a job that relies mainly on technological skills, I would be much more interested."

One of my references told my prospective employer that I was fired from my last job for excessive absenteeism. How do I handle that fact on an interview?

Explain that your last job did not work out because you missed too much work. Give the reasons: "I was caring for my sick mother," or "I was going to law school at night," or "I lost interest in the job because I had been doing very repetitive work for over three years." Stress that now you are in an entirely different frame of mind; either you have resolved your problem or you feel this new job will give you the challenge you are looking for. Make it clear that coming to work every day—even staying overtime—will not present any problems to you.

I was out of work for eight months and have a gap on my resumé that interviewers always ask me about. What can I do?

Be as honest as possible. Explain that you had a hard time deciding what your next step should be, and took your time before accepting a new position. You used those months in a constructive way by taking a course or two, practicing your word-processing skills, volunteering at your local hospital, and so on.

ELPFUL RESOURCES

WEB ADDRESSES	PUBLICATIONS
www.rileyguide.com by Margaret Riley, career writer	**How to Read a Financial Report** by John A. Tracy
www.dbm.com by Drake Beam Morin, career consultants	**Knock 'Em Dead 2000** by Martin Yate
www.jobhuntersbible.com by Richard Nelson Bolles	
www.sunfeatures.com by Joyce Lain Kennedy, (noted career columnist)	
www.latimes.com/class/employ/	
http://content.monster.com/jobinfo/ **interview/questionstoask/**	

Refining the search

A stalled search 108
Take a good look at yourself

Interviewing review 110
Revise and refine

Check your tactics 112
Perhaps there's a smarter way to proceed

Adjust your focus 114
On the wrong track altogether? Swerve

Find support 116
Isolation can hobble your hunt

Consider relocating 118
Not for everyone, but sometimes it helps

Now what do I do? 120
Answers to common problems

Remember, there's the distinct probability that all your job-hunting efforts will land you in a better job than you've ever had before.

a stalled search

Is it the job market? Something you've said or done?

On a morning like any other, you do what you've always done. You put your key in the ignition of your car, you turn the key, and instead of an engine roaring to life, you get this: click ... click ... click. You wonder whether it was something you did, like leaving the lights on. Or something that had nothing to do with you, like a mechanical defect, an act of vandalism, or the subzero weather. Bottom line is, you need an answer. Turning the key in the same old way is just not going to work.

As a job seeker, it's not uncommon to run into a similar scenario. You send out resumés, follow up on leads, keep up with your network, and suddenly you're no longer getting results. The phone is not ringing. You're not being invited back for second interviews. You get the feeling your e-resumés are being launched into a void. What to do?

Call in the mechanics to help you locate the source of the problem. Find a job counselor you feel you can trust—at school or work, or in private practice—to look over all your presentation materials and assess your performance as a prospective employee. Review your job-hunting strategies and your plan of action. Call the people you've listed as references and double-check what they are saying about you (see next page). In other words, identify the factors that are gumming up the works.

HAUNTED PAST

Some companies hire firms that specialize in checking the backgrounds of job applicants. They look up your motor vehicle, criminal, and credit records. They verify your address, social security information, and your former supervisors' comments.

If your past is haunting you, don't let it surprise a prospective employer. Tell interviewers about any problems that are likely to show up in a background check, and assure them that you've resolved those problems, or reformed your character, repented, or somehow turned around whatever negative situation they may turn up.

Meanwhile, you might want to review the references you are giving to prospective employers:

■ Have you talked to or met with those people lately? Do you know for sure that they could recommend you based on your past performance?

■ If you haven't worked in the same area for a time, have you updated people you have chosen as references about your recent accomplishments?

■ Is it possible that any of them might not be able to comment positively on your future potential?

review your interviewing skills

Evaluate your difficulties, write off your losses, and refine your job campaign

As you begin to overhaul your job search performance, direct your attention first to the quality of your physical presentation. At interviews have you appeared well-pressed and healthy? Do you smell good? Do your clothes look like you're headed for a day in a business office? If there's any suggestion that you could be on your way to the beach or out to the driveway to wash your car, you've got a problem.

A rule of thumb for interviews: dress like a bank president. It's better to dress up than down. Save trendy, individualistic, cutting-edge fashion statements for your free time.

Next, evaluate your typical interview behavior. Stage a pretend interview with a friend. Ask him to give you honest feedback about your interview style. Ask this informal critic if your tone of voice, overall attitude, handshake, eye contact, friendliness, and accessibility are acceptable.

Does your critic tell you that you come across as a person confident of his own abilities? Are you enthusiastic about the position, or just pretending to be interested? Do you keep up a two-way conversation, or have you monopolized the interview? Did you sit there like a bump on a log? Were you overly familiar?

Review your resumé and cover letters. Ask a friend who is in business to look at them again. Is the resumé the best representation of you that it can be? Is it free of typos, errors of fact, grammar, syntax? Is it typed on high-quality, white bond paper, clean, and unwrinkled? Does your cover letter highlight your past successes in overcoming obstacles and convey what a hardworking, creative, ambitious individual you really are?

# ASK THE EXPERTS

I can't get past the screening interview. Could it be my breath?

Maybe, which would be a terrible shame, wouldn't it? But it's so easy to correct next time with toothpaste, flossing, and mouthwash. Consider avoiding spicy foods, garlic, and onions before the interview, as well. Another interview-ender: too much cologne or perfume. The sense of smell is very subjective—your favorite scent may drive the interviewer to the brink or give her a sinus headache. Better to refrain altogether.

Despite my best efforts, my cover letter often spills over to two pages, sometimes more. Is this a problem?

If you think about the big stack of ad responses facing the person screening your resumé and cover letter, then you have your answer. Keep the cover letter short—three paragraphs or four at most—and relevant to the job in question. Mention the job you're applying for, then in two or three sentences say why you're a good candidate, citing the skills you have that match up with the requirements of the job. Include contact information, and indicate how you will be following up. And then stop.

I'm very shy and nervous around new people. What can I do?

Practice interviewing with a friend. Ask for feedback about any nervous habits you may be displaying: facial tics, sweaty palms, coughing, involuntary grimaces. Once you're aware of them, you can regain control. Next, query your friend about whether you are fully answering questions posed by the interviewer. Practice responding in ten sentences or so. Get comfortable with telling little stories about yourself, your abilities, things that happened to you at your last job. Rehearse, rehearse, rehearse. Then, if you can enlist a friend of a friend who does not know you very well, role-play the same scenario and ask for a fresh critique.

check your tactics

Stay in the hunt, even if you must change your methods

You're doing great. Remember, hunting for a job is one of the most stressful situations in a person's life. Take good care of yourself while you're hard at it.

Insomnia is a common complaint of job-hunters. Regular exercise and well-balanced meals can help to ensure sound sleep at night.

Many people keep on target by treating the job hunt as if it were a 9-to-5 job. They wake up early, clip job ads, respond to job leads, conduct research on new industries and jobs, work on their networking skills, talk to a certain number of contacts each day, arrange informational interviews, attend association meetings and professional seminars, and, hopefully, go on interviews for prospective positions.

Other people find such a regimen too demanding. They prefer to break up the weekly routine of the job search by making time for a tennis lesson here, taking a computer class there, visiting a sick relative, volunteering at a local charity, or doing errands that they once reserved for busy Saturdays. They may work on their job hunt in the morning and keep their afternoons free.

You need to find the rhythm that works best for you and your temperament. What's important is to find the best way to keep your spirits up and to stay on track toward the future you are working to create for yourself.

BEATING THE REJECTION BLUES

The main problem with job hunting is having to live with rejection. It's part of the job search. It can be doubly upsetting if you have a long wait before finding out you didn't make the cut for a particular position. Not only do you not get the job, you may just never hear from the interviewer at all. (No one likes to be the bearer of bad news, so interviewers seldom get back to candidates to say "You didn't get it." They hope the candidate will get the idea eventually. It isn't nice, but it happens.) So remember:

1. In most instances the reason you do not get any given job has nothing to do with you personally. Office politics, the boss's daughter, cancellation of a project— there are so many reasons that you were not hired that there is no point in concerning yourself with them. Just get on to the next possibility.

2. Understand that anyone you meet while job hunting can become a valuable contact later in your career. So consider the hunt part of networking and try to enjoy getting to know people you meet during your job search.

3. Remember, there's the distinct probability that all this hard work will eventually land you in a better job than you've ever had before.

FIRST PERSON   SUCCESS STORY

Stop the downward spiral

After I was laid off, my bills started to pile up, and I began to lose sleep. Soon I was so worried that I could no longer concentrate on writing letters for my job search. I sat watching TV all day. At an interview a friend had wangled for me, I stuttered with anxiety and could not concentrate on the interviewer's questions. Finally my wife called our family doctor because she thought I was making myself sick. Thank goodness he understood what I was going through. He suggested that I try an over-the-counter sleeping medication and a half hour of exercise every day. Well, it worked like a charm. After a few nights of sound sleep and some early morning walks, I was my old self. I started cranking out the letters again. I aced my next two interviews and now have a better job than I did before.

John R., Minneapolis, Minnesota

adjust your focus

You may be pursuing a strategy that makes no sense

Once you're sure the pieces of your presentation fit together nicely and your job hunt is efficient, it's time to review your overall strategy. Given what you have learned so far about the job market in your chosen field, are you going after the right job? A stalled search may mean that you are looking in a field that isn't right for you.

For example, what if you are rather shy and reserved but have your heart set on getting out of sales support into sales. Your quiet demeanor may tell interviewers that you're not sales material.

Or it may seem obvious that full-time work isn't for you if you tell the prospective employer that you are attending college at night, caring for two preschoolers (and a husband), but you are looking for a more challenging full-time position. Or perhaps you've mentioned that your parents are not in good health and often need your assistance.

Generally interviewers shy away when you talk about your outside responsibilities. Perhaps they think you're overdoing things and might be pulled away from the job by personal problems. Maybe they're right. This may be the time to ask about flextime, telecommuting, job-sharing, or other part-time scenarios.

Perhaps you are feeling burned-out with your career as an account executive, and it's showing in every interview you go on. At your last interview, instead of talking about your work goals, did you talk about how you have always dreamed of running your own business? Well, this may be the time to start.

Realize that your job hunt may be backfiring for a reason—your strategies may not be the right ones for you at this time of your life. Your current lack of success could actually provide the impetus for you to examine new directions.

Quiz   WHAT'S BUGGING YOU—
YOUR JOB OR YOUR COMPANY?

	True	False
If you are conducting your job hunt while keeping the job you have, these questions may help you determine if you are on the right track. Answer true or false:		
1. My work still interests me, but my boss has never appreciated me.		
2. I never felt that I was a good fit with this company.		
3. I can do this work with my hands tied behind my back. There must be more to life than this.		
4. I can't stop thinking about whether I could open my own business.		
5. I can't seem to get ahead at my company. Everyone says my work is good.		
6. I have a lot of years invested in this industry now, but I feel so burned-out. Besides, the company's not doing well either.		
7. I can't remember the last time I enjoyed what I was doing.		
8. I work with the nicest people anywhere, but I need a change.		
9. I need to do more and feel I am capable of more, if only someone would give me a chance.		
10. I am disillusioned with my company's philosophy and the way its employees are treated.		

You should consider a different type of job if you answered True to questions 3, 4, 7, and 8.
You need a similar job in a new company if you answered True to questions 1, 2, 5, 6, 9, and 10.

find support

*Job hunting
is tough on
the psyche*

Feeling like a fish out of water? It's understandable.
Job hunting is not part of the everyday world—working is. So give
yourself a break and seek out other landlocked fish for some moral
support.

There are well-established groups that have developed tried-and-
true methods for helping people while they are out of work. Forty
Plus, for instance, is a nationwide non-profit network for older
executives looking for jobs that has branches in many cities.
Members receive job search training—including practice interviews—plus assistance with resumés, career counseling, networking, and support groups. Look in the white pages of your phone
book to see if there's one in your area.

Other places to inquire are community centers, adult education
centers, colleges, churches, and synagogues. Or you might start
your own group at one of these places by advertising for other job-
hunters in the want ads or on community bulletin boards.

Support groups also may be found in the *National Business
Employment Weekly*, in its "Calendar of Career Events." If the publication is not on your newsstand, it can be ordered from P.O. Box
435, Chicopee, MA 01021-0435 (or call 800-JOB-HUNT, ext. 193).
Or look in the yellow pages under Careers.

If group situations make you nervous, find a career counselor to
help you through this very trying process.

TRY A COUNSELOR

Career counselors can pry you out of funks and help you solve the problems that may be sabotaging your interviews. Think of a career counselor as a personal trainer, someone who is part expert, part coach.

Fees for career counseling differ in various areas, but they run about the same as for marriage counseling or personal counseling, anywhere from $50 to $100 an hour. Counselors sometimes offer group sessions that are reasonably priced. Such groups meet regularly to share ideas and experiences and to role-play interviews. If you are part of a group laid off from the same company, your outplacement benefits may include professional career counseling and possibly related support groups, as well.

Here are some indicators of a qualified counselor:

1. The counselor charges by the hour (including a fee for the introductory interview).

2. There are no up-front payments or contracts committing you to a course of payments.

3. On the initial interview you meet the counselor you'll be working with instead of a salesperson.

4. The counselor has a degree in social work or some other related field (see box).

consider relocating

Maybe get a whole new life?

Maybe you need a serious change. Not just a new job, but a whole new everything—house, scenery, friends. Or perhaps you've been offered a job out of state. Is it worth it? Here are considerations to mull over before you institute a move, with all its uncertainties and expenses:

✓ How does the cost of living compare to where you are now? A salary offer in another area may seem astronomical (or ridiculously low), until you find out about rent, food, taxes, and tuition costs there.

✓ How will you get to work? Do you hate riding a bus or train? Or does driving a car every day make you wish for the convenience of public transportation?

✓ Factor in the weather. Do you get blue during a long winter? Wilt in 120°F summers? Love the changing of the seasons? Hate endless days of rain?

✓ Don't forget lifestyle: Do you enjoy gardening? Cultural events? Outdoor sports? Intellectual pursuits? Can you easily get to ski slopes or beaches, the mountains, or a lake?

✓ Will you miss old friends—or are you looking for a new crowd? Will you be near enough to your family?

THE COST OF MOVING

This is not an inexpensive option. The minimum cost of moving an average-sized houseful of furniture is $10,000 for just a short distance. Then there are broker's fees to sell your old house, closing costs for a new house, hotel fees during the move, and possibly furniture storage fees if you don't find a new house before you move. It may take you several years to break even after incurring such expenses.

If you already have a job in a new location, perhaps the company can be persuaded to help you with the moving expenses. Don't look to Uncle Sam for much help, however; tax breaks are slim for relocation costs.

HAT'S OUT THERE: RELOCATING

INTERNET ADDRESSES

www.homefair.com
Covers all aspects: schools, crime stats, cost of living

www.monster.com
Comprehensive look at relocation and what's involved

www.wsj.com
Articles on living and working abroad

BOOKS

Places Rated Almanac: Guide to Finding the Best Places to Live in North America
by David Savageau and Richard Boyer

Jobs '00 (annual)
by Kathryn Petras et al.

U.S. Department of Labor
Regional information on salaries

Chamber of Commerce
Local unemployment figures

now what do I do?

Answers to common problems

What if I don't think I want a full-time job after all?

Companies will sometimes agree to splitting one job between two employees, both of whom work on a part-time basis. For example, one works Mondays, Wednesdays, and Fridays, and the other works Tuesdays and Thursdays. Often the idea to divide a job in this way originates with the employees themselves. A selling point for the employer may be a savings in the cost of fringe benefits—one or both of the employees may not qualify for health benefits. To succeed, sharing a job requires that both employees develop a foolproof method for communicating with each other so that pieces of projects do not slip between the cracks.

My job counselor keeps telling me to give up accounting and try sales, but I think it's demeaning work. What should I do?

Job counselors are good at matching personalities with various jobs. She may be seeing a side of you that you aren't aware of. If straightforward sales seems too much for you, maybe you should consider marketing accounting firms or selling new accounting services.

I'm running out of cash, and the only job offers I've gotten are jobs I don't want. What do I do?

This is a tough call. You must consider that the job you really want may take longer to attain than you thought at first. You may have to do some stopgap work in the interim. But do think about whether your job goal is realistic.

I get the feeling lately that I'm looking for the wrong job.

You may be. We all are, at one time or another. First, check yourself. Are you still interested in your chosen field? Try doing some of the self-discovery exercises in Richard Nelson Bolles' *What Color is Your Parachute? 2000*—good for identifying your skills as well as the best industries and positions for you. If you're still confused, get out of the house and do temp work for a while, at as many different types of jobs as you can get. Try sales, maybe, and then clerking, and then working in a medical environment. Temp in as many different fields as you can. One of your temp jobs may open up a whole new world. And you'll make new friends who will have new contacts and leads for you to explore.

ⒽELPFUL RESOURCES

WEB ADDRESSES

www.latimes.com/class/employ/
More tough questions

www.entrepreneur.com
Focus on small business owners

www.careermag.com
Site covering all aspects of job hunting and alternatives

www.careers.wsj.com
Online career counseling

www.score.org
Service Corps of Retired Executives, all volunteers offering free advice to new business owners

www.monster.com
Chat rooms on relocation

www.nbcc.org
National Board of Certified Counselors

www.wsj.com
Wall Street site featuring articles on Career Topics

Job offers

Evaluating the job............................ 124
Is this the right one for you?

Negotiating salary........................... 126
There is a right way to ask

Evaluating benefits.......................... 128
Their value can be significant

Negotiating benefits......................... 130
You may get more than you think

Accepting an offer........................... 132
Put yourself in the picture

Updating your network....................... 134
Get the word out about your new job

Turning down an offer....................... 136
Close the door gently

Now what do I do?........................... 138
Answers to common problems

Nirvana!
You've reached an agreement with your future boss about your salary
and benefits package, and you're both happy with yourselves
and each other. You shake hands—and then what?

W E L C O M E

A B O A R D !

evaluating the job

The company is great. Hopefully the job is too.

The long-awaited moment has arrived. You've been offered a job! Your new would-be boss just called to express his interest in hiring you and asked if you could meet him tomorrow to discuss your compensation package. You are incredibly excited. And relieved. And scared.

But wait a minute. How much do you know about this company? What's more, this could be the greatest place in the country, but if the offer you are getting is not suitable for you at this time in your career, you could be aching to leave within months.

You have informed yourself about the company to some extent, or you would not have gone for an interview. Now's the time to inform yourself more fully, and specifically evaluate whether this is the right place for you. Be honest about your expectations, inclinations, dreams, and ambitions. Here are questions to consider:

✔ Is the track fast enough? Are you on the fast track, expecting to rise quickly in the company? Find out how rapidly this typically happens in the job you have been offered.

✔ What sort of work space will be assigned to you? Do you like solitude and quiet? A cubicle may not encourage you to produce your finest work.

✔ Do you care about the company's product? Can you sincerely devote yourself to this work? Or are widgets the last thing in the world to hold your interest?

✔ Is this job a good career move for you? Will you gain new skills and knowledge that someday will catapult you into a senior management position? Will you be satisfied to stay a year or two, make some money, and then move on? Will this job pay more than your last one, even though it might fail to challenge you?

MORE QUESTIONS TO PONDER

■ Is this company a start-up or is it well-established?

■ Has there been much job turnover at the company recently?

■ Are the employee benefits considered generous or stingy? When would you be eligible for them?

■ Is this a large company or a small one? Which size would be more suitable for you?

■ Will you like the day-to-day duties of your job?

■ Will the job make good use of your skills?

■ Is the location one where you can live easily on your salary?

■ Will the company give you any training or opportunities for advancement?

■ How often will your performance be reviewed?

■ If you stay with the company, what's the next job you might be promoted to after this one? Do you want it?

WHO MAKES THE OFFER?

The prospective boss may do it, since she is the person who will be working with you, and it helps her to build an immediate bond with you. However, some companies like to leave the salary offer in the hands of a human resources representative, who can answer specific questions on company policies and procedures. Other companies may let the boss make the offer and the HR representative brief the prospective employee afterward.

negotiating salary

What to ask for, and how to get it

You've reviewed all the relevant factors, and you are certain that this is the job for you. Now you want to get the best salary you can. But how do you go about it? Here are some guidelines:

✓ If you have been smart about your job hunt, you have done your homework on salary levels for the position you want. To do that, you studied the salary surveys on the Internet for your job, your industry, and your location, so you will know what range your position will fall into. If you have not done your homework yet, check out the Web sites. Knowing what the salary standards are for the job you're seeking will give you an edge during the negotiating process.

✓ Find out what part of the company's annual raises is based on cost-of-living increases (i.e., likely to come to you automatically) and what part is based on merit. Ask about the annual schedule for awarding both, and how long you must work at the company to be eligible. You also might ask for a special early review if your starting salary is below industry standards. A low salary can be more palatable if you obtain a promise of a compensation review in, say, three to six months.

✓ If you are offered a salary that you feel is not suitable, explain why you feel you deserve more. Point out the norms for the industry and the area. Describe your special attributes, such as years of experience and special skills.

Above all, remember the adversary during the negotiation process may be your future boss. Negotiate carefully. It is best to be open to some compromise so you both feel you're coming out as winners.

HAT IF

The salary is low but I've been promised a high bonus?

Make sure you understand what the bonus will be based on. Are there specific business goals you need to reach? What will happen if you reach only 60 percent of your goals? Try to get the boss to spell out all the contingencies. And try to get the details in writing. Remember, when you are eligible for a bonus, the person who's promising you everything may be working in another department, or even another company, by bonus time. Also, you shouldn't think the terms for a bonus are an annual deal; next year you'll have to renegotiate.

The boss refuses to talk about whether the company has annual raises?

This should be a signal to you that something is not above-board in this company. You are asking legitimate questions that deserve some kind of answer. Trying asking him to clari-fy—are there raises only if performance merits it? Are there any cost-of-living increases? Is there any information on salary reviews in the company handbook?

You overstated how much you were making before? Will the prospective employer find out?

He may and he may not, depending on how thorough his reference-checking people are (see page 85). If he does, though, you're probably not going to be considered for the job. If you do run the risk, you could prepare a logical explanation in case you are asked about the discrepancy. Perhaps you could say you were including the value of the company's bene-fits. Or just admit that you exaggerated because you felt you were substantially underpaid and worthy of more.

(see page 85)

DOS AND DON'TS FOR NEGOTIATING SALARY

Do know your market value (study industry surveys beforehand).

DO ask about stock options, tuition reimbursement, extra vacation pay, moving and relocation allowance, travel budget, seminar attendance, and perks like a laptop or cell phone.

DON'T get nasty, con-frontational, aggressive, accusatory, or arrogant.

DO let the prospective employer know that you really want to accept an offer at his firm, if only you can agree upon the specifics.

DO get the offer—and all the extra perks—in writing.

evaluating benefits

These extras can amount to 25 to 50 percent of your salary

This portion of your compensation can put money in your pocket—or take it out. So pay attention to what the person in human resources tells you. The basic benefits usually include the following:

➤ Time Off: The number of holidays can range anywhere from nine to twelve, and employees are usually given two or three personal days as well. (If you observe non-Christian religious holidays, ask about the company policy regarding these.) Vacations typically start with a minimum of ten days. New hires are often required to work at least six months before they can take a vacation for the year. (If you are hired close to summer or toward the end of the year, ask how flexible this policy is.) The number of vacation days can increase the longer an employee is with the company. Ask how many years it takes to work up to fifteen days and twenty days.

➤ Disability and Workers' Compensation: A percentage of your salary continues if you are injured off or on the job. The company pays the premiums.

➤ Health Insurance: A traditional insurance combination of hospital and major medical covers inpatient hospital stays and emergency room care, outpatient care in a doctor's office, pharmacy bills, and lab costs. Or an insuring organization, such as an HMO or PPO, may provide these services within a preferred list of health-care providers. Some companies offer one type of health insurance; others offer a choice. The company typically picks up part of the premium, and the employee pays the rest. Check to see what your share will be.

EXTRA BENEFITS

Mid-sized and large companies usually offer a range of additional benefits. These can enhance your personal life, as well as raise the dollar value of your compensation. Consider the following:

Pension or retirement plan: The company contributes money to a Defined Benefit Plan for you, usually a percentage of your salary.

401(k) or 403(b): These are tax-deferred plans that allow you to defer a portion of your income directly into retirement accounts without paying tax on that amount until you retire. The company often contributes additional money to your account as well.

Life insurance: The company may buy coverage at a multiple of your salary. If it's twice your salary of $50,000, your beneficiaries will receive $100,000 if you die while employed. You may be able to buy additional coverage at a reasonable rate.

Accidental Death and Dismemberment insurance: This coverage pays a benefit to you or your heirs in case you suffer grievous injury. The award is a multiple of your salary.

Miscellaneous benefits: Larger companies may offer other benefits, all of which can add significantly to your compensation package. Consider these: vision and dental insurance, transit-checks, tuition payment, maternity and other family leaves, sabbaticals, and assistance with counseling for both job problems and personal or family difficulties.

Day care services: Child care can be one of the heaviest burdens for working parents to manage. If you need dependable help, a good company program could be a deciding factor in your job hunt.

negotiating benefits

Sometimes bargaining can boost your earnings

Benefits can get even richer. Some companies give additional compensation to certain employees as a matter of course, and others may give it only if you ask. If your prospective boss won't budge on a low salary figure, try negotiating for extra benefits. Here are a few of the options you should ask about, especially if the standing offer is less than ideal:

Bonuses: A bonus is often awarded to an employee at the end of a project or at the end of the year. Ask when bonuses are customarily awarded to employees, how much they are, and how you might qualify. If there is a shortage of workers with your skills in the industry, but the company can't offer a competitive salary when you're hired, you might ask about a signing bonus. It's a one-time cost they may be able to justify in their budget.

Profit sharing: In many firms these plans cover all employees, usually awarding a percentage related to your base salary. Ask how the percentages are determined and if the award goes into a fund held until you leave the company. (If you will be steering a major project, you also might negotiate for a percentage of its profits, either in the form of a bonus or additional profit sharing.)

Dues, expenses, and tuition for professional associations and training: Your membership in professional associations and travel to industry conventions could benefit your personal career as well as your company. The company also might find it valuable to pay your tuition for courses that improve your skills or lead to a degree.

Company car or paid expenses for your own car: If your work requires you to drive, be sure to find out if you will qualify for subsidized transportation or if the company will furnish you with an automobile.

NON-MONETARY EXTRAS

There may be ways for the company to reward you that will not show up in your paycheck, but will save you money or give you more satisfaction. Consider asking for these if you want to augment a low salary:

Extra vacation days: Some companies have very stingy policies about salary, but are more flexible about awarding vacation days. At executive levels and sometimes even at middle-management levels, additional weeks might be negotiable.

Flextime or space: If a firm will let you off, say, every Friday afternoon to coach your child's soccer team, you could be more amenable to less-than-ideal compensation. Similarly, you might find the base salary more acceptable if the company allows you to telecommute one or two days a week from home, cutting down on the time and expense of your transportation.

accepting an offer

After you say yes, settle the details

future boss about your salary and benefits package, and you're both happy with yourselves and each other. You shake hands—and then what?

Before going home to celebrate, get a road map for your new job:

🗝 Discuss your starting date. If you're working, it's advisable to give your current employer at least two weeks notice so she can make plans to replace you. If you give less, your new boss will surely make a note of it and may question your professionalism.

🗝 Ask your new boss what she expects from you during the first six months of employment, and how you can best prepare to hit the ground running from your first day forward.

🗝 Inquire about who will train you. Will the boss or another team member do it, or will the person you are replacing stay a few days or weeks to break you in? If it's the latter, ask to meet that person and arrange a lunch together.

MATERIALS YOU NEED

Here's some homework to better prepare you for your new job:

Job description: If you don't already have your job description, ask for it now so that you can see how your duties are described and prioritized.

Organization chart: A look at how the organization works will help you to get a handle on company hierarchy and your place in it.

Corporate handbook and newsletters or bulletins: These are usually available in larger corporations. They can help you understand policies and the company's values. The periodicals will give you a taste of the corporate culture: what's acceptable, what's humorous, what's political, what's touchy, and what's absolutely verboten.

Try to get a glimpse of your new workspace when you've accepted a job offer. That way, on your first day at work you can bring whatever will make you most comfortable—framed pictures, desk accessories, tissue box, plants. You also can visualize what it will be like to work in that space. You may then want to request any special accommodations you need—a step stool, perhaps, or an ergonomic chair.

updating your network

Convey your thanks to those who have given you help

After you've been on the job for a week, it's time to contact people who have been involved in your job search. Let them know they have been instrumental in helping you land this job, fill them in on the details of your new responsibilities, thank them from the heart, and make it plain that you're ready to return the favor.

Who to call? First, call those people who furnished references for you. While you're thanking them, you can inquire about their conversations with your boss—what type of concerns did he voice about your past performance or your abilities? Did he indicate the direction he hoped to take his department? Was there any indication of how your predecessor fared in this position?

Next, get in touch with people who gave you information, leads, and contacts that led to the new job. Let them know they were successful in helping you. Feed them any information about the company that you can share without compromise—positive, non-confidential news they may find interesting. Offer to serve as a contact in the future for someone else they might want to refer.

Finally, don't forget people whose assistance did not, in the end, lead to the job you finally landed. After all, their efforts were important because they were intended to help you. Tell those people about your new job, and thank them for their efforts on your behalf. Let them know you are available to assist them.

Sure, networking takes time and effort, but you cannot afford to neglect it. Since 50 to 70 percent of all jobs are filled via networking, you definitely want to put your energies into keeping yours up, even when you are employed and not immediately seeking another position. Besides, some of your networking pals may turn into close friends, another valuable asset.

SK THE EXPERTS

How do I keep my network going?

Many people start monthly meetings with colleagues over lunch or after work to keep in touch. Periodically phone or e-mail each person and tell them what is going on in your part of the industry. Get better acquainted with their careers and ambitions. And attend farewell parties, social events, industry meetings, and conventions. When possible, help people by returning favors.

What's the best way to build my network?

Start by renewing contact with former bosses and colleagues. Identify contacts you'd like to have, at a company you've targeted as your next possible move, for example, and figure out who can introduce you to them. Give talks at professional meetings or write articles for industry newsletters. To keep up with developments, consider joining a job search network that publishes job vacancies and market information for your industry (www.netshare.com, www.searchbulletin.com, www.execunet.com). If you are an executive, work to establish ties with board members of companies you're interested in (consult their online Web sites).

GET THE WORD OUT

Return to professional association meetings and announce your new position. Consider putting a notice in your alumni newsletter or professional bulletin. The more people who hear about your work and keep up-to-date about your career, the better. Everyone loves to be associated with a winner. Your new job identifies you as someone who is desirable in your industry. That kind of reputation can ease the next move in your career.

turning down an offer

Close the door very gently— you never know where these contacts will turn up again

Chances are if you decide not to accept a given job offer—for whatever reason—you are going to meet the people involved somewhere again in your career or deal with the company again in another capacity. Later on you may even want to work there. So take care when turning down an offer.

Even if you have no intention of coming near a particular company or prospective boss ever, ever again, don't let your aversion show. Turn down any job offer graciously, even reluctantly. After all, your candidacy for the position in question has been considered with great care. It is only fair for you to show that you have given that offer serious consideration in return. This is not to suggest that you lie about why you are not taking the job. But the reason for rejecting it can be stated in a way that will not offend.

➽ Is the salary too low? Saying "You can't possibly expect me to work for such a piddling salary," will reflect badly on your professional acumen. Instead, perhaps you can put a positive spin on the situation by saying something like, "It's a great job and I love the ideas you have, but I have to earn more than you're offering in order to pay for my child's tuition."

➽ Is the position no real promotion for you? Don't insult them with "This would be a real comedown for me." Instead, try to imply what you really want: "I think the world of your project, but I'm hoping to move to a managerial level in my next job."

End your conversation with a compliment, perhaps, "I hope we have an opportunity to work together somewhere down the line." It may give you a reason to stay in touch and perhaps be another addition to your network.

SK THE EXPERTS

Suppose I get an offer, but I'm really interested in another job? Should I accept the first offer and then cancel it if the second one comes through?

You could, but that is considered very unprofessional. It is far better to ask the first company for some time to think over their offer; then call the second company and tell them you're very interested in them. Ask when they will make their decision. Mention that you've had an offer and have to give a final answer within a couple of days. Stress again how much you would prefer to work for their company. If time runs out on you, reconsider the first job and decide if it really is the right one for you or if maybe you should keep looking.

I started a new job two weeks ago, and it's not at all what was described to me. Meanwhile, I've received an offer from another company I had interviewed with months ago. What's the most professional thing for me to do?

Request a meeting with your current boss and explain your confusion about your role. See if there is a satisfactory explanation for the discrepancies between what you were promised and what you are encountering. If you decide the job was misrepresented, politely give your notice (the company may not require much, since you've been there a very short time). But be sure to ask a lot of questions about the new job offer before you give notice so you won't wind up in the same situation again!

now what do I do?

Answers to common problems

I have planned a two-week vacation this summer and have non-refundable tickets. The hitch is, I want to change jobs before then. How do I handle this?

Wait until a company expresses serious interest in you and asks about your availability. Then tell them about your vacation plans and inquire if it would be a problem for you to take the time off, unpaid, of course. Depending on the dates, they may prefer to have you start after your vacation. Don't worry. This would rarely squelch a deal. Companies understand that people have lives and make plans in advance. Just be honest.

I'm trying to choose between two jobs and need to know which one has better possibilities for promotion. How can I find this out?

Study the company in general and the department in particular. Are job openings posted on bulletin boards or on the company's intranet to make employees aware of open positions? Does the company tend to look for outside talent when filling higher-level positions? Ask about the work history of middle and senior management—did any of them rise up through the ranks? Find out if your performance will be reviewed regularly. Is there a career path already in place for your particular job? For example, do data entry clerks often move on to customer service jobs and from there to sales positions?

Can I ask for more money after I've been working for a few months?

You can always ask for more money. Just be prepared to justify your request. Do some research into competing salaries for similar jobs to make your case stronger. Be ready to show what your contributions have been. But if you are turned down, be gracious. State your basic satisfaction with the company and find out when you can expect to have a formal performance review and merit increase.

Should I ask about benefits before I start working, or wait until my first day on the job?

It's perfectly understandable that you want to know about your benefit package before accepting an offer. Ask to speak to the human resources department, which can give you all the latest and most accurate information. Make sure to ask when you are eligible for benefits—for example, you may need to continue your current health insurance plan for a few months until the new coverage kicks in.

HELPFUL RESOURCES

WEB ADDRESSES

www.workforce.com
Executive compensation

www.forbes.com
Executive compensation

www.careerperfect.com
Relocation surveys, salary information

www.insweb.com
Insurance benefits

PUBLICATIONS

Encyclopedia of Associations
Gale Research, Inc.

Business Periodicals Index
Articles on companies in the news

U.S. Global Trade Outlook Global growth prospects (published by the U.S. Department of Commerce)

Monthly Labor Review Projections for 200 industries (published by the U.S. Bureau of Labor Statistics)

The Smart Woman's Guide to Interviewing and Salary Negotiations
by Julie Adair King

Negotiating Your Salary: How to Make $1000 a Minute
by Jack Chapman

On the job

You did it, now what?! 142
You have to face that first day at the office

Settling down 144
A checklist for the first week

Fitting in 146
Find out how the game is played

Getting along 148
Taking your place in the office family

Staying out of trouble 150
Don't blow it

Getting ahead 152
Make the long haul worth it

Now what do I do? 154
Answers to common problems

A grasp of the big picture will help you plan
your strategy for advancement.

you did it, now what?!

A few tricks to surviving your first day fluster-free

Was it Woody Allen who said that 80 percent of success is showing up? He neglected to mention how weird that first day on the job can feel. There's just no way to get around it—think of it as a rite of passage. You worry about how you'll learn every name, location, policy, and procedure.

Remember riding a bike for the first time? Your full attention was on the task at hand, and you didn't give up until you had mastered it. You learned by doing. By the end of the day, you were squeezing those brakes instead of slamming them, and could even make U-turns without falling off. And you were only six years old!

Today, you're again making history in your own life and at this company. You'll always remember this day. Proceed with the same concentration you gave your new bike at age six, and you will make a success of this chapter in your career.

Why is this chapter here, anyway? What's this got to do with getting a job? Well, this has to do with keeping your new job. Otherwise, you'll be returning to page 1.

HOW TO CREATE A POSITIVE IMPRESSION

Everyone at the new place will be forming their first impression of you when you go to work. Since a first impression can last awhile, you want yours to be the best it can be. It never hurts to:

Look Great: Wear a nicely tailored suit, polished shoes—a clean neat appearance. Remove evidence of body piercing. Avoid fashion statements, punky hairdo, Elvira makeup, blood-red stiletto fingernails, and too many splashes of your favorite perfume or cologne. Iron those shirts and blouses and comb that hair. Beards and mustaches should be well-trimmed too.

Act Great: Be polished and professional. Be accessible. Greet everyone you meet with warmth and enthusiasm. Don't act like a know-it-all. Instead, try to strike a balance between being confident—you got the job for the reason that you are good at what you do—and humble—there's a lot to learn about doing your job in this place and with these people.

Be Grateful: Thank your boss for her confidence in you. Tell her how excited you are to be with the company.

Be Positive: Decide you're coming back tomorrow, no matter how confusing the first day might be.

settling down

*Learning your
way around*

Getting through the first week is an exercise in keeping your head. It is not going to be easy, but every day will get better. Take things a step at a time:

Day 1: Paste a big, warm smile on your face and shake hands with everyone you meet. Go to lunch with the boss (if invited). Remind yourself that you don't have to learn everything you need to know on this day. Take plenty of deep breaths so you won't seem anxious.

Day 2: Set up your workspace. Orient yourself to the office layout—find out which closet holds the office supplies and learn who orders the supplies you don't find there. Inquire about where the lunchroom is. Talk to your coworkers to get a feel for the place. Ask if taking breaks is customary here or if the habit is frowned on.

Day 3: Read any company literature you can lay your hands on that you didn't get during the hiring process (brochures, manuals, employee guides, strategic plans). Study the table of organization to understand the company hierarchy.

Day 4: Familiarize yourself with the company's products or services. See if you can sit in on any departmental meetings. Visit other departments if you can. Ask questions, but don't make a pest of yourself.

Day 5: If you haven't met with your boss to formulate short-and long-term plans of action up to this point, try to get it done today. Also, if you have bottom-line responsibilities, ask your boss for a copy of the departmental budget. This document can help you understand restrictions on spending and staffing for upcoming projects. (It also will help you discuss the strategic plan with your boss so that you see where the company is headed and how your unit fits.)

THE HUMAN RESOURCES DEPARTMENT

HR will officially welcome you to the company by inundating you with buckets of paper. They'll warn you to fill out everything (especially your W-4 form) or you won't be put on the payroll! You can get a head start on your first day by bringing the following to work with you:

■ Proof of eligibility to work in the United States (passport or birth certificate and a social security card; for non-citizens, a green card or appropriate visa).

■ A voided check to facilitate the direct deposit of your paycheck.

■ In a large firm HR is likely to invite you to an orientation session to familiarize you with the company's ways and give you a copy of the employee handbook and the policy and procedure manual. Ask for information about holidays, vacation, personal days, and sick leave if you didn't go over it during your hiring process. See if they can give you a floor plan of the whole office and a table of organization. Find out if there is an annual picnic or Christmas bash, and put it on your calendar.

■ Make friends with the folks in HR and visit them often—they are your window into the company. They can help you not only in interpreting the policies but in adjusting to the corporate culture in general.

MAKE A NOTE

Get a job notebook and take notes about everything—legible ones that you can read back during the coming days and weeks—so you won't have to ask to be shown things over and over. Of course you think you will remember how to do what you are shown—nothing that you are learning is tough—but you won't. Even the simplest procedures will drift away as you try to absorb all the new information during the first few days. Particularly important: write down passwords for computers, e-mail, electronic gateways, and other security information.

fitting in

Observing the corporate culture will make your new job go smoothly

How do you get acclimated as quickly as possible?

You play by the rules. Simply put, you demonstrate RESPECT for the company's policies and procedures, hierarchy, supervisors, coworkers, clients, and vendors. The company's way of doing business needs to become your own. This may mean being at your desk fifteen minutes early, wearing conservative clothing, relating calmly and professionally to customers with a complaint or coworkers with a grudge, or simply coming to work with a smile and a friendly, approachable demeanor and positive outlook. The short of it is, you need to play by their rules, not your own.

But you also need to play to win. What does that mean? It's understanding your position in relation to others—your place in the grand scheme of things, how your contributions (or lack thereof) can spell success or failure for the company.

Then you take it a step further. Do more than you are assigned, ask questions, learn about the next step, then take it. Emulate your superiors and aim to acquire the skills that have made them successful. Stay in a continual learning mode, watching and listening, signing up for additional courses. Do your best to find a mentor to advise you on your career.

IF YOU'VE GOT A FEW SUGGESTIONS

Now, suppose you have some great ideas. Do you tell your boss how to run the company, save money, service customers in a more efficient manner? No. Save your suggestions until you have established yourself as a solid citizen of the company whose word can be trusted. And how do you come to be a trusted employee? By meeting deadlines on all assignments, maintaining the highest standards for yourself and your work product or service, having all your ducks in a row, AND getting along with everyone by being personable and professional. Then you will be recognized as a known and trusted commodity—one the company will not part with voluntarily. Then your suggestions will be listened to with interest—not before.

FIRST PERSON **DISASTER STORY**

New man out

A few years ago, I landed an entry-level job in a small architecture firm in Connecticut. I loved their designs and felt honored to be part of their team. To my dismay, I was fired after only six months—they said I was "not fitting in." I realize now I made a bad first impression that I could never really overcome. To begin with, I came in late twice the first week. I was involved in community affairs and had to meet with the town supervisor about a fountain I wanted to design for the town center. Then I took a walk during my lunch hour rather than eat with the others in the lunchroom. Finally, I talked to my boss as if I was his equal, telling him how he could improve his business. I guess I just didn't show much respect for the company.

Norman W., Brooklyn, Maine

getting along

Some people at the office require extra special care

It's Monday morning and, by some twist of fate, the train pulls in to your platform on time and deposits you at work a few minutes early. You are in a pretty decent mood for a Monday until ... you run into a few of your office mates, and they start with the same backbiting comments you heard last week.

As with your real family (Mom, Dad, sisters, and brothers), you did not get to choose these characters at the office. Yet you have to live with them, understand and tolerate them, in order to work together with them in a team toward a common goal, whether it's making more money for the company or improving service to your customers or producing a better mousetrap.

Do you have to love this family? No, thank goodness! But after a while you may find that you develop, in spite of yourself, a great deal of affection for them.

If you have trouble keeping up pleasant relationships with people at the office, look around you. Is there someone who's a master at it? Take a good look at how that person behaves and do likewise. It isn't just a skill worth learning—it's worth its weight in gold.

Guidelines for Problem-Solving in Your Office

Here are some sample problems and possible ways to handle them:

Problem: The secretary does not greet you in the morning.

Problem: Your complaining coworker chews your ear off.

Problem: Your supervisor hasn't commented on your progress report.

What Not to Do:

Don't take things personally! AND *Don't* take any of these problems to management! The last thing most supervisors want is to deal with such behavior. This is not what they think they are getting paid for.

Consider this: She may feel that the office is not a place to socialize. Or perhaps she fails to realize that greeting coworkers is normal office etiquette, as is allowing others to get to know her. Or you may remind her of her younger sister who laughed at her for taking schoolwork seriously.

Consider this: He has trouble with authority figures owing to his hypercritical stepfather. Although very bright, he's never been given a promotion.

Consider this: She once had your job. She's unsure of herself in her new role and thinks acting haughtily is appropriate. She lives in fear that her promotion will be taken away from her—as her mother warned—and that she will be unmasked as an imposter.

Do what you can to settle the problem yourself. Compliment the secretary on her good work; share a sandwich with her in the lunchroom; tell her you feel hurt when she doesn't say hello.

Do what you can to settle the problem yourself. Encourage your coworker to take courses and expand his horizons; join his friends in helping to steer him toward a more positive frame of mind.

Do what you can to settle the problem yourself. Reassure your supervisor that you are a team player trying to make her look good; pass on information that will help her anticipate the company's needs.

staying out of trouble

DO YOU KNOW HOW YOU CAN SHOOT YOURSELF IN THE FOOT?

	TRUE	FALSE
OK, now is the time to find out if you get the picture. Test your savvy about office procedure by answering the following questions true or false.		
1. Never come in early or your boss will expect you to be early every day.		
2. Volunteer for more work and you'll be expected to do more for the same salary.		
3. You should ask your boss to spell out your responsibilities and put them in writing.		
4. Don't talk to coworkers—you're here to do your work and that's all.		
5. Have a glass of wine or a beer at lunchtime. It will calm your nerves and you'll work better.		
6. Look for someone knowledgeable in the company to be your mentor.		
7. Go over your boss's head to get noticed by the higher-ups.		
8. Feel free to dress in the way that expresses your true inner self.		
9. Tell your boss you want to do it your way.		
10. Refuse to do anything that is illegal.		
If you answered True to 3, 6, and 10, you've got the picture. All the rest are false. If you got more than two answers wrong, reread this chapter.		

HAT IF

You need to investigate and observe. Does this person react to everyone in his line of vision in a similar fashion? Perhaps he only communicates with staff of a certain stature—managers and above. Maybe he's not a morning person. Or he has no idea who you are and why you are trying to start a conversation with him. Check it out with your colleagues. If he's known to be a friendly guy, and it's just that he doesn't know you, look for an opportunity to be formally presented to him. If that's already taken place, try reminding him (later in the day) with some comment such as, "Hello, Mr. Jones, I'm Sara Willis. I just started working in the art department. I read your comments on the economy in the *Washington Post* yesterday. Did you feel you were accurately quoted?"

It's a good idea to find out during the first week what your job entails, what is expected from you in terms of output, and how you are expected to accomplish the goals that have been outlined for you. Read over that job description again. Make sure you understand the nature of the duties described. Then attempt a brief meeting with your boss to go over your responsibilities and decide upon a timetable. Try to establish deadlines and the form your reports should take. Work out with her the best means of communication between the two of you: face-to-face meetings, video conferencing, cell phone connections, e-mail, notes left on her desk, etc. If you can't see her in person, send a memo or an e-mail outlining how you propose to proceed and ask her advice. Also inquire if you've left anything out.

getting ahead

A grasp of the big picture will help you plan your strategy for advancement

Look closely at your company. Do you basically agree with what your company stands for? Do you respect the product or service it provides? Study how your company treats people—inside and out. If you like what you see, great—you're in sync!

Next, try to understand the big picture at your company—how the different pieces fit together, how your small role influences the final outcome and how it reflects the company's mission, objectives, and future direction. That way you can plan where you want to be next. With a firm grasp of the big picture, you might be able to suggest a strategy that will advance the company mission while creating an opportunity for yourself.

Research the top managers' backgrounds and education. Would you like to emulate the career path of someone in senior management? Can you pay the price of doing what she had to do to get where she is today? If possible, sit with her and discuss her career while charting your own. Then try to gain similar experience yourself. If you feel comfortable with the way she manages her career, ask her to be your mentor (see page 76).

Take steps to demonstrate your potential, whether by volunteering for special projects or suggesting ways to improve the company's systems, products, or services. Anticipate the next steps in your assignments and perform them without being asked. Try to work out solutions to current problems instead of expecting others to find them. Identify something that needs to be done, then do it. Demonstrate daily your ability to learn and grow, to be a resource person for others, to become a can-do, make-it-happen manager in your industry.

Once you meet performance expectations, plain old likability may help to get you where you want to go. Attracting mentors, teachers, and networking buddies, as well as gaining the reputation with your peers of being "easy to work with" are essential. Never ever underestimate the power of your people skills.

TAKE STOCK OF YOUR WORK HABITS

If you are not getting ahead at work, it could be because of you, the company, or your boss. Before you blame the company or the boss (or other coworkers), consider these common personal faults.

Do you put things off? Try always doing the biggest, ugliest 400-pound gorilla of a chore first. You are going to have to do it anyway. Get it over with, and you will have saved all that time you've used in the past to pussyfoot around big, hateful projects. Then you can spend that newly gained time doing something you really like.

Is your office—and your job—in a mess? Disorganization can sap your effectiveness. Try putting everything out of sight (even if you have to cadge another file cabinet from the company). Then take out only the one—ONE—most pressing project that you must finish today. When you finish, take out the next project. Don't worry about what's in the file cabinets until you complete the project on your desk.

Do you let things slide? Miss deadlines? Try keeping a journal of every single thing you do for about three days. That includes phone calls to your mom, e-mail orders for your son's jeans, planning the community picnic, and answering questions about the computer for your colleague in the next office. See just how much time during the day you are spending on activities that have nothing to do with the project you must complete. Take stock—honestly—of how many of those activities you should save for after work or during lunch hour. Block out periods of time when you won't allow those activities—or any others—to interfere with the project you need to finish. And then concentrate on getting it done.

now what do I do?

Answers to common problems

How long do I have to stay at one job? I don't want to look like a job-hopper.

Short answer: two years minimum. Anything less will make the next company skittish—they'll conclude that you're just looking to get your ticket punched and move on quickly. Longer answer: In certain fields (like computer technology), employees are hopping around wildly because salaries are rising astronomically and current employers are having a hard time keeping up with outside offers. Before you move, weigh pros and cons—money is only one factor in determining your degree of job satisfaction.

I'm the only African-American in my department in a company that is not very culturally diverse. How do I fit in without selling out?

"Speak the language of your environment," is the advice of Dyan Doughty-Kelly, the African-American principal of an organizational consulting firm, ABINTRA, in Philadelphia. "As an African-American, you have to make people comfortable with you. Once they are comfortable with you, they get comfortable with your differences."

People at my new job assume I've got a lot more experience with computers than I do. What should I do?

If there is a huge discrepancy—they think you're a programmer, but in reality, you can just about find the start button—you need to confront the fact that this is not the right job for you at this time. Did you misrepresent yourself during the interview process? If the gap is not that wide, discuss with your boss your need to brush up skills in Excel, for example. Or is there a super computer whiz in your department who can get you over the rough spots? Find out without delay.

What's the best way to attract the positive attention of management quickly?

Try any and all of the following: innovative ideas, shoulder-to-the-wheel mentality, taking the initiative, chipping in when obstacles need moving, a hands-on approach, ease at getting along with others (to name a few).

I'd like to take a course to help me with my new job. What's the best way to go about it?

Discuss your current and future needs with your boss. Seek advice from your company's human resources department. Find out if your company has a tuition reimbursement plan which could help you defray some of the cost of any courses you'd like to take.

My first-year job review is coming up. Is there anything I should do to prepare for it?

Take some time (an hour or two) to review what you've accomplished your first year. Jot down any major project you have completed, others you've started, money you've saved the company. Note, too, the things you didn't do and the things you want to do. (Big companies may even have employees fill out a self-appraisal before their review.) The point of all this preparation is, when you meet with your boss, you should be prepared to fill in any information that is missing from the discussion that might be advantageous to you. The preparation also should help to prevent you from being totally surprised by any criticism you receive.

I haven't had a performance review in two years. What should I do?

Ask for one. It's how you get raises.

ELPFUL RESOURCES

WEB ADDRESSES	PUBLICATIONS
www.careermag.com	**From Making a Living to Having a Life: A Book for the Working Challenged** by Gloria Dunn
www.altavistacareers.com/ articles/upward.html	
	Callings: Finding and Following an Authentic Life by Gregg Levoy
	Leadership from the Inside Out by Kevin Cashman
	Corporate DNA by Ken Baskin

Be your own boss

Instead of a job 158
Try the road less traveled

Do you really want to be on your own? 160
You need to be honest about the way you like to work

Working at home 162
The solitary path to profits

Running a business outside your home 164
For the most intrepid entrepreneur

Being a freelancer 166
Still working for corporations, but at your own pace

Now what do I do? 168
Answers to common problems

Suppose you want to find a different way out of this
wilderness of job hunting. There is an alternative—a rocky path
that's mostly untraveled because it can be precarious and uncertain
—self-employment.

instead of a job

Why not strike out on your own?

Suppose you want to find a different way out of this wilderness of job hunting. There is an alternative—a rocky path that's mostly untraveled because it can be precarious and uncertain—self-employment. But as one wise man said years ago: "Paths are made by walking." If you know deep down that you are more of a pathmaker than a follower in other people's footsteps, then self-employment may be the right course for you.

More and more people are choosing to go into business for themselves. Computer power, the World Wide Web, and e-mail make many of these small-business ventures easier to operate. E-commerce also allows a mini-company to reach out over vast territories, combing for customers in need of their products or services.

How can you make sure that self-employment really does suit your temperament? First, ascertain whether you have something to sell: a product or a service. Reliable market research can help you determine whether or not there is a demand for it.

Then you'll want to determine whether or not you have the skills needed to manage your own business. If not, you'll need to find out how to acquire them.

Another important key to success is sufficient capital to see your business start-up through. A solid business plan indicating how long-term growth will be achieved [see page 163] can help you determine just how much capital you need.

Another invaluable item you'll want to have on hand is a full Rolodex™ of contacts. One part of it should be devoted to a strong network of advisers; it's important for you to learn from other people's mistakes—and from their triumphs too. A different section should be full of freelancers who can help you plug the gaps if your business starts to boom.

And perhaps the attribute that comes closest to ensuring your success: you need to have a personal responsiveness to your customers' needs.

Quiz	DO YOU HAVE THAT ENTREPRENEURIAL SPIRIT?	True	False
Here's a quiz to determine whether or not you're suited to working on your own. Answer these questions true or false:			
1. I often need a push to get started in the morning.			
2. I don't like taking directions from others.			
3. At the end of the day, I like to put thoughts of work aside and concentrate on my hobbies.			
4. I can make decisions quickly and without too much worry about the outcome.			
5. I don't have much patience when things don't go my way.			
6. I'm one of those people who enjoys keeping track of things, filing, and record- keeping.			
7. For some reason, people usually don't trust me until they know me better.			
8. I would just as soon let others take charge.			
9. I've been told that I am a good motivator.			
10. I prefer not to work directly with people.			

If you answered True for questions 2, 4, 6, and 9, and False for all the others, you can claim a healthy entrepreneurial spirit. If more than four of your answers were different, maybe you should think again. Self-employed people succeed most often if they are entrepreneurs. That means they like to take charge. They're decisive, diligent, good with people, talented at organizing, and persuasive. The most successful are also persistent, and incredibly hardwork-ing. If you don't have all these qualities, you need to team up with someone who has the ones you're missing.

do you really want to be on your own?

Check the water before you dive in

Consider the following pros and cons that people who are self-employed have compiled. If you are wild about the pros and can manage to live with the cons, this may be the way you should go.

PROS:

- Lots of time on your own with little structure

- Flexibility—you work when you want to work

- You make all the decisions

- You take orders from no one

- No limit to earnings potential—your level of income depends on you, not on office politics, or whether your boss likes you, or the fortunes of a corporation.

CONS:

- None of the social interactions of an office environment (lunches, breaks, after-work friendships)

- No work equals no pay. That not only includes days when you are sick but personal days and vacations as well.

- No paid benefits. You have to purchase your own health care and disability insurance, invest in your own pension, etc.

- No bonuses, or other praise for your accomplishments.

- Constant pressure to sell your product or service—to "hustle." These marketing requirements will take significant time away from the development of your product or the rendering of your service.

- Need to do all administrative and maintenance work yourself—billing, ordering supplies, repairing equipment.

- No steady paycheck. If a client company decides to take its time paying your bill, you usually have few alternatives except to wait … and wait … and wait. And you must realize that you will occasionally have a deadbeat client.

- No 9-to-5 work schedule. You can find yourself working twenty-four hours a day if you aren't careful.

WHICH BUSINESS?

The logical choice for your self-employment is a business you know, because you won't have to spend time getting up to speed learning a new line of work. Most people who are successfully self-employed establish their new business as an extension of a job they already have done for a corporation. They simply take the skills they have learned and mold their business around them. For example, an accountant may leave her job as assistant to the treasurer at a big company to advise small firms on how to manage their financial affairs. A practical nurse might give up working for a convalescent home to establish a temp service for home health aides.

Some fields show more promise than others. According to futurist predictions, the following list details ten employment fields that are expected to be the fastest-growing during the twenty-first century. If your self-employment falls into one of these categories, you are likely to enjoy an added advantage.

Computer support	**Investment and financial**
Engineering	**services**
Health care	**General management**
Home care	**Retail**
Marketing and Sales	**Social work**
in e-commerce	**Education**

These categories also might be profitable industries for job-hunters to explore. Also see page 15.

Also see page 15.

working at home

*If you are
a self-starter,
read on*

There you are, curled up comfortably in a corner of your abode, working on your laptop. Your favorite music's on the stereo, a hot mug of java's nearby, and your cat's in your lap. You're wearing your p.j.'s and your hair's uncombed. You take breaks when you feel like it (to pick up your child from school, attend a concert, play a round of golf). Sounds like a swell way to make a living, doesn't it?

There's only one catch. You have to enjoy working alone. Working from home can be isolating, and many people find they miss the give-and-take among office colleagues. But if that won't bother you, proceed.

First you need a product or a service that you can develop and sell from your home—and sell well enough to support you and your dependents. Publishing a financial newsletter, maybe? Or writing magazine articles? Then you have to make sure your product or service is up-to-date. That means you'll need to study industry trends, including the development of new product lines or services in your area of expertise.

You'll need to do your research on the business aspects. Consult with friends or relatives who have experience working at home to see what they like about it, and what they don't like. Interview small business entrepreneurs, whether they work at home or in their own offices, to unearth the pitfalls of running a business yourself. (Your financial outlay is likely to be considerably less than if you start a business outside the home.)

Then you will need to initiate your marketing. Acquaint yourself with demographic information about your customers by frequenting the stacks of your nearest business library. Call businesses you have worked for and with and find out if you can sell your products or services to them. Get your business onto the Internet, either by creating your own Web site for it or getting it listed as part of an associated site. It also could be helpful to join relevant trade associations, possibly the local small business association and/or the chamber of commerce.

MAKING A BUSINESS PLAN

A good business plan is essential to the success of your entrepreneurial endeavor whether you want to be a writer in your home office or sell goods from your garage. It forces you to think about the assets you will need to succeed in your new venture. If you've never tried to formulate a business plan for yourself, have no fear—there is nothing mysterious about it. It simply requires good sense and thinking ahead a little. Just write down answers to the following questions, and you will have the workings of a basic business plan:

■ What are the benefits you will offer to your customers?

■ Can you describe the marketplace for your service or product? Is there a need for it? Are there other products already being sold that might fill that need?

■ How would your service or product beat the competition? Or fill a unique need?

■ What do you need to perform the service or produce the product you will be selling? Workspace? Equipment? Storage? Extra utilities? Part-time or full-time employees? Business services such as accounting, legal advice, or delivery help? How much will all this cost?

■ How will you sell your service or product? Writing letters, mailing brochures or catalogs, establishing a Web site? How much will these sales efforts cost? (Remember to count your time as an expense.)

■ Can you determine your break-even point? In other words, how much do you need to sell each month to cover your expenses?

■ Try to project how much you are going to sell in the coming year. Do you see any growth potential in your business for the years ahead? Will demand for your service or product continue to rise, stay the same, or will it wither? Will you be able to raise your fees or prices if expenses go up?

running a business outside your home

You'll need the right resources

There are ways to be your own boss without starting from scratch. You can buy an established business or purchase a franchise (the right to start a branch of an established company—usually a retail business).

Buying a business takes money. You'll need to consider how you can secure the financing; will it come from your own savings, from family and friends, from banks, or from venture capitalists?

Buying a business is a lot easier if you have good legal advice. Before you sign anything, you will need to ask your lawyer to look over the contract. Consider the restrictions in a franchise contract: you may be locked into the franchiser's list of suppliers, their advertising budget, their standard operating procedures.

The counsel of experienced small-business owners can be invaluable. Ask your business contacts for their informal appraisal of the business or franchise you are considering. Is the product a good one, worthy of your investment? Will you be dealing with a recognized trademark? Does the company have a solid business reputation?

You will find yourself saddled with many additional responsibilities and tasks. Are you flexible enough to learn quickly? Perhaps the most important skill you will learn is how to manage people. Do you have any natural ability in that area?

Before buying a business or franchise, you will need the wholehearted emotional support of your friends and family. It is smart to consider very carefully the demands of buying a business—not only what it will cost you but what its effect will be on those around you.

CHOOSING A PARTNER
WHO MEANS BUSINESS

Acquiring a partner who can help you shoulder the burden can be beneficial to a new business start-up, especially if you choose someone whose talents and skills complement rather than duplicate your own. In fact, the main reason for having a partner is to find someone who is good in areas in which you have no expertise.

Your business partner must share your values and support your goals. He or she also should have compatible personality traits. Most of all, you should agree on money issues, such as how much income to reinvest in the business versus how much to spend on salaries.

Put every aspect of your partnership agreement in writing. The process of working out the agreement can help you hammer out exactly what your individual responsibilities are going to be. Be sure to spell out how and when the partnership can be terminated.

FIRST PERSON   **DISASTER STORY**

Financial planning?

My cousin and I were thrilled to be able to sell our services as interior designers for business spaces. We made over her garage as a workspace, and almost killed ourselves to get our first jobs done on time so that our customers could move into their new offices. We were written up in the local newspaper, and after that we were busy all the time. But soon we noticed that our customers let their bills slide for months. We didn't want to make a fuss, because so many of our sales are based on recommendations. We started borrowing to cover expenses until the bills were paid. At the end of the year our accountant was furious with us. She explained that we should have printed on our invoices: "Payment due in 30 days—1.5% interest on payments after 30 days." That would prompt customers to send their checks on time, and if they did not, the interest would pay for the loans we needed in the meantime. We lost some of last year's profit due to the cost of borrowing money, but now with our new invoice forms, the checks are coming in sooner, so with our savings we're moving to our own new space.

Ron A., Chicago, Illinois

being a freelancer

*Getting paid
by the hour or
by the project*

What about selling your skills instead of a product? If you have been writing speeches for your boss, you might want to present yourself as a freelance speechwriter to other companies. If you put together parties for the promotion department of a big corporation, you might try organizing wedding receptions or special events.

First you need to know if your skills are current and whether there are companies or individuals out there who will pay you to work for them. Then you become not an employee, but an individual who is renting himself out for an agreed-upon rate to perform certain tasks, complete a project, or assist in reaching specific goals.

Welcome to the freelance world!

You do a job and you get paid for it. There are no entanglements, no future promise of employment—and you are free to walk away when you want to do something else. There are also no regular paychecks, paid vacations or sick days, nor medical or retirement benefits.

This can be an easy, footloose style of living, a way of generating income using your best skills while pursuing your other interests (acting, going to school, writing a bestseller, traveling). Or it can be a harrowing way to live, because you must be constantly on the lookout for your next assignment. It all depends on you, your temperament and orientation, and your commitment to make it work. As with all self-employment, you must know yourself and answer this question honestly: Can you tolerate taking risks?

Then you must do the research. Seek advice from other consultants who have been successful in the business. Using your existing network, approach people with your services who already have an appreciation of your abilities and talents. Build up a client base from these people, and follow up by calling them regularly to keep in touch. Ask for their word-of-mouth recommendations. Also, advertise in professional journals, business periodicals, and on your own Web site.

WHAT'S THE DIFFERENCE?

There are various ways to work in this freewheeling style:

Freelancer: You sell your skills or services and you charge by the hour, the day, or the project. Example: A freelance copy editor who charges $22 an hour and is called when her clients need her.

E-lancer: You have sophisticated computer skills and work as a freelancer on the Internet. You charge by the hour or by the project. Example: An e-lancer designs Web sites for business owners, colleges, or online magazines. He communicates with clients and sends most of the work by e-mail, with periodic planning sessions on-site.

Contractor: You usually work in a company side by side with regular employees on a time-limited project. You may be paid by the company or by a temp agency (see page 61). Example: An accountant is hired by a company to help out while the accounting system is being revamped.

Consultant: You offer managerial services on an hourly or project basis. Example: A time management consultant or an organizational development consultant assists senior management in making strategic decisions about a company's work habits and staffing requirements.

 ## WHAT'S OUT THERE

Web Addresses

www.fastcompany.com
Start-up archives

www.dbm.com/jobguide/misc.html
Self-employment info

Publications

The Lifetime Career Manager: New Strategies for a New Era,
By James Cabrera and Charles Albrecht

Now what do I do?

Answers to common problems

As a freelance graphic designer, how do I know how much to charge for my work?

If you have worked for a company as a graphic designer, add up your former annual salary and the cost of buying your benefits (medical premiums, retirement annuity payments, disability insurance). Divide the total by the number of hours you work during the year. Then compare the hourly rate you come up with to those you find on discussion lists or chat rooms that address your particular profession, such as at www.lizst.com or www.tile.net/lists. Search www.asae.com for a professional association that caters to designers. Talk to professionals in your field to get the most current information on what the market will bear. Attending local professional association meetings also can keep you up to date about fees. But in the end, be prepared to negotiate hourly rates.

Is there an association that can help me get started in my own business?

The Service Corps of Retired Executives (SCORE) has an excellent reputation, vast resources to draw upon, and an excellent Web site (www.score.org). Check out their discussion groups and sign up for their free monthly e-mail newsletter. You also can request two free brochures from their local chapters: "A Guide to Office Efficiency" and "A Guide to Setting Up Your Home Office."

How do I find an agency to place me in temporary work as a proofreader?

Look in your local newspaper's agency listings for a firm that specializes in publishing. Call generalist temporary agencies as well to see whether they handle the kind of assignments you desire. These sources also will give you an idea of what rate of pay to expect. Try cold calls to publishing companies you have researched to see if you can interest them in your services—you may be able to get a better rate of pay on your own. Follow up with a lively cover letter and your resumé.

I've borrowed most of the money I need for starting my own business from family members. Where can I go to get more capital?

Prepare yourself: most start-ups need to tap into savings, credit cards, loans against 401(k)s or insurance policies, home equity loans, or other liquidation of assets to finance the business. If you decide to approach outside sources, you will need a first-rate business plan (check out Internet resources listed opposite for help with this). Banks will require collateral for any business loan—your home, your boat—so you will be putting your possessions at risk if you decide to go to them for money. Venture capitalists in your area will be interested if you have a business idea that promises aggressive profits, but if you take their money, you will lose some control over your business. Try to pick one with a good track record.

Do I need an attorney to go into business for myself?

These days you need an attorney to cross the street! You certainly need the best advice you can get on setting up your business legally and in compliance with all existing legislation regarding safety, equal employment opportunity, and filing requirements. You'll need an accountant too, for rules of incorporation and tax regulation.

HELPFUL RESOURCES

WEB ADDRESSES	PUBLICATIONS
www.2h.com More personality tests	**Mastering the Art of Creative Collaboration** By Robert Hargrove
www.careermag.com All topics	**Teaming Up** By Sarah and Paul Edwards
www.entrepreneur.com All topics	
www.wetfeet.com/asp/home.asp All topics	**The Fast Forward MBA in Project Management** By Eric Verzuh
startup.wsj.com Help in formulating a business plan	**Everything You Need to Know to Start Your Own Small Business** By Paul Resnick
	Entrepreneurial Finance By Richard L. Smith and Janet K. Smith

index

A

accidental death and dismember-
    ment insurance, 129
accountants, 169
acquaintances/friends
    borrowing money from, 168–169
    employment with, 66
    networking and, 70–71
    as references, 85
    relocating and, 118
action verbs, 31, 35, 36
adaptability, 25
ads
    college career services and, 56–57
    by job-seekers, 67
    online, 54–55, 67
    print, 52–53
    radio or television, 66
    recordkeeping and, 64–65
advancement opportunities, 124,
    125, 138
    strategy for, 152–153
age
    asking about in interviews, 93
    associations for seniors, 57
    skills and, 26
Albrecht, Charles: *The Lifetime
    Career Manager*, 167
alcohol, 150
Allen, Woody, 142
annual reports, 63
appearance, 89, 104, 110, 111
    first day on the job, 143
application forms, 86
aptitude tests, 10–11
    employment agency, 58
    exploring dreams with, 14
arrest records, 93
artisans, 11
artists, 27
ASCII, 42
attention, attracting, 154
attorneys, 169
authority, respect for, 95
automobile expenses, 130

B

background checks, 108–109
Baskin, Ken: *Corporate DNA*, 155
benefits
    asking about in interviews, 91,
    93

    evaluating, 128–129
    freelance employment and,
    166–167
    negotiating, 130–131
    in salary negotiations, 127
    self-employment and, 160
    when to ask about, 138
blind ads, 53
Bolles, Richard Nelson: *What Color
    is Your Parachute? 2000*,
    15, 121
bonuses
    negotiating, 130
Boyer, Richard: *Places Rated
    Almanac*, 119
burnout, 114
business, starting, 158–169
    buying established, 164–165
    capital for, 158, 161, 168–169
    choosing a partner for, 165
    selecting a business, 161
    skills for, 161
Business Periodicals Index, 139
business plans, 163

C

Cabrera, James: *The Lifetime Career
    Manager*, 167
*Callings: Finding and Following an
    Authentic Life* (Levoy),
    155
capital, 158, 161, 165, 168–169
career changes
    evaluating desirability of, 80
    resumés for, 38, 48
career counselors
    college career services and,
    56–57
    exploring dreams with, 14–15
    fees of, 117
    finding certified, 117
    following advice of, 120
    stalled job searches and, 108
    as support, 116–117
Career Exploring on the Internet
    (Gabler), 67
career moves, 124
career services, 56–57
Career Xroads (Crispin, Mehler),
    49, 67
Cashman, Kevin: *Leadership from
    the Inside Out*, 155

Catalyst, 153
chambers of commerce, 119, 162
charity, networking in, 73
chronological resumés, 34, 36–37
classified ads, 52–53
clothing
    for first day on a job, 143
    for interviews, 104, 110, 111
cold calls, 78–79
college career services, 56–57
cologne, 111
communication skills, 21
    in a new job, 151
community centers, 116
company literature, 144
competition
    in business plans, 163
    at interviews, 85
computer skills
    desirability of, 21
    electronic resumés and, 42–43
    importance of, 16
    improving, 17
    on resumes, 40
confidentiality, 43, 55
conscientiousness, 95
consultants, 167
work schedule of, 19
*A Consumer's Guide to Retail Job-
    Hunting Services*, 15
continuing education programs, 23
    computer skills and, 17
contractors, 167
corporate culture
    interview impressions of, 99
    new jobs and, 146–147
    researching, 62
Corporate DNA (Baskin), 155
corporate handbooks, 133
correspondence courses, 23
cost of living
    relocating and, 118
    salary increases, 126
cover letters, 44–47
    customizing, 46–47
    importance of, 44
    long, 111
    no-no's in, 45
    reviewing, 110
coworkers
    dealing with, 148–149
    interpersonal skills and, 9
Crispin, Gerry: *CareerXroads*, 49, 67

Crystal-Barkley Corporation, 15

D

day care services, 129
degree programs, 23
demand, skills to meet, 20–21
Dictionary of Occupational Titles, 62
direct deposit, 145
disability insurance, 128
disabled persons, 27
    associations for, 57
    interview questions about, 93
discussion lists, 54
diversity, 154
DOS text, 42
downsizing, 48
dreams, 12–13
    exploring, 14–15
    reality and, 12, 13
Dunn, Gloria
*From Making a Living to Having a
    Life*, 155

E

e-commerce, 158
education, 22–23
    career services by, 56–57
    in computers, 17
    describing in interviews, 90
    networking in, 73
    on resumés, 32, 36, 38, 40, 48
    tuition reimbursement, 130, 155
Edwards, Sara and Paul: *Teaming
    Up*, 169
e-forms, 43
e-lancers, 167
electronic resumés, 42–43
*Electronic Resumes and Online
    Networking* (Smith), 43
e-mail, resumés via, 42–43
employers
    expectations of, 132–133, 151
    as mentors, 77
    skills valued by, 20–21
employment agencies, 58–59
    fees for, 59
    interview follow-up in, 99
    unresponsive, 66
employment history
    dealing with in interviews,
        92–93
    explaining poor, 108–109
    gaps in, 26

on resumés, 36
Encyclopedia of Associations, 105,
    139
enthusiasm, 25, 27
    in interviews, 95
Entrepreneurial Finance (Smith,
    Smith), 169
entrepreneurial spirit, 159
*Everything You Need to Know to
    Start Your Own Small
    Business* (Resnik), 169
executive recruiters, 60–61
exempt work, 19
experience
    describing in interviews, 90–91
    gaining, 25
    lack of, 24
    negative, 24
    in a new job, 154
    rating, 24–25
    on resumés, 31, 32

F

fidgeting, 87
first day in new jobs, 142–143
flexibility, 164
flextime, 18, 114
    negotiating, 131
Forty Plus, 116
403(b) plans, 129
401(k) plans, 129
franchises, 164–165
freelance employment, 166–167
    networking in, 79
    work hours and, 18, 19
friends. *See* acquaintances/friends
*From Making a Living to Having
    a Life* (Dunn), 155
full-time employment, 18–19, 114
functional resumés, 34, 38–39

G

Gabler, Lori: *Career Exploring on
    the Internet*, 67
goals
    describing in interviews, 96
    in a new job, 151
    reality and, 12–13
    setting, 12–13
grooming, 110, 111
guardians, 11
The Guide to Internet Job Searching
    (Riley-Dikel, Roehm), 43

H

Hargrove, Robert: *Mastering the Art of Creative Collaboration*, 169
headhunters, 60–61
health insurance, 128
high-end ads, 53
hobbies
  as potential careers, 13, 15
  on resumés, 33
holidays, 128
How to Read a Financial Report (Tracy), 105
How to Survive and Prosper As an Artist (Michels), 27
human resources departments
  beginning a new job and, 145
  interviews in, 84–85, 87

I

idealists, 11
income, 18–19
  accepting unwanted jobs for, 120
  blind ads and, 53
  bonuses, 127
  exempt vs. non-exempt, 19
  raises, 126, 127
  rejecting inadequate, 136
  salary negotiation, 126–127
  salary surveys, 62
  self-employment, 160
industries,
  booming, 15
  lagging, 15
informational interviews, 74–75
  cold calls for, 78–79
  questions to ask in, 75
initiative, 53
insomnia, 112–113
insurance, 128, 129
interests
  determining, 8–11
internships
  for career changes, 80
  locating, 80
  research through, 63
  on resumés, 40
interpersonal skills
  importance of, 9
  in interviews, 88–89, 94–95
  in a new job, 148–149

teamwork, 21
interviews, 82–105
  basic information in, 90–91
  behavior before, 86–87
  describing employment problems in, 104–105
  difficult questions in, 96–97, 104
  dressing for, 104, 110
  etiquette for, 89
  evaluating impressions from, 99
  follow-up after, 98–99
  grooming for, 110, 111
  illegal questions in, 85, 93
  informational, 74–75
  interpersonal skills for, 94–95
  preparation for, 96–97, 103
  process of, 84–85
  psyching out interviewers, 88–89
  recordkeeping for, 65
  references and, 85
  research before, 62–63
  second, 102–103
  subjects to avoid in, 92–93
  thank-you letters for, 98, 100–101
  unspoken questions in, 95
invoices, 165

J

Jebens, Harley: *100 Jobs in Social Change*, 27
job descriptions, 133
  clarifying in interviews, 91
  researching, 62
Job Finder's Guide (Krantz), 67
job offers, 122–139
  accepting, 132–133
  accepting unwanted, 120, 137
  benefit evaluation in, 128–129
  benefit negotiation in, 130–131
  evaluating, 124–125
  multiple, 137
  pre-planned vacations and, 138
  salary negotiations in, 126–127
  at second interviews, 103
  turning down, 136–137
  updating network about, 134–135
job resources, 50–67
  career services, 56–57
  contacts, 64–65

employment agencies, 58–59
headhunters, 60–61
online ads, 54–55
print ads, 52–53
research, 62–63
jobs
  avoiding trouble in, 150–151
  first day in, 142–143
  first week in, 144–145
  fitting in at, 146–147
  getting ahead in, 152–153
  getting along with coworkers, 148–149
  how long to remain at, 154
Jobs and Careers with Non-Profit Organizations (Krannich), 27
job search clubs, 14
job searches
  changing focus in, 114–115
  cold calls, 78–79
  length of, 9
  recordkeeping in, 64–65
  reevaluating stalled, 108–109
  reevaluating tactics for, 112–113
  refining, 107–121
  relocating in, 118–119
  support in, 116–117
  while employed, 115
job sharing, 19, 114, 120
Jobs '00 (Petras), 119
job turnover, 125

K

King, Julie Adair: *The Smart Woman's Guide to Interviewing and Salary Negotiations*, 139
Knock 'Em Dead 2000 (Yates), 105, 121
Krannich, Ronald: *Jobs and Careers with Non-Profit Organizations*, 27
Krantz, Les: *Job Finder's Guide*, 67

L

language
  in interviews, 88
  on resumés, 31, 35, 36
Last Minute Resumés (Toropov), 49
Lauber, Daniel: *Professional's Job Finder*, 27

Leadership from the Inside Out (Cashman), 155
leadership skills, 20
learning, 146. *See also* education
letters of offer, 131
Levoy, Gregg: *Callings: Finding and Following an Authentic Life*, 155
life insurance, 129
lifestyle preferences, 118
Lifetime Career Manager, The (Cabrera, Albrecht), 167
listserves, 72
low-end ads, 53

M

management skills, 8
    desirability of, 20
manners
    before interviews, 87
    in interviews, 88, 103
marketability, 16–17
marketing, 162
Mastering the Art of Creative Collaboration (Hargrove), 169
math skills, 21
MBA programs, 73
Mehler, Mark: *CareerXroads*, 49, 67
mentors
    choosing, 77
    evaluating, 81
    finding, 72, 76–77
    professional meetings and, 72
Mentorship: The Essential Guide for School and Business (Reilly), 81
Michels, Carroll: *How to Survive and Prosper As an Artist*, 27
motivational skills, 20
moving
    considering, 118–119
    cost of, 118
multitasking skills, 20
Myers Briggs Type Indicator (MBTI), 11

N

National Certified Career Counselors (NCCC), 117
National Certified Counselors (NCC), 117

National 4-H Club, 80
National Mentoring Partnership, 80
negligent hiring, 85
Negotiating Your Salary: *How to Make $1000 a Minute*, 139
negotiation skills, 21
nervousness, 86–87, 111
networking, 68–81, 113
    cold calls and, 78–79
    gaining experience through, 25
    getting the word out with, 70–71
    information interviews for, 74–75
    maintaining, 135
    mentors and, 76–77
    at professional meetings, 72–73
    updating about job offers, 134–135
newsletters, 133
non-exempt work, 19
non-profit organizations
    for career changes, 80
nutrition, 112–113

O

objectives, on resumés, 33, 36
100 Jobs in Social Change (Jebens), 27
online ads, 54–55, 67
online research, 63
organization charts, 133
orientation sessions, 145

P

Parker, Yana: *Ready to Go Resumés*, 49
partners, selecting, 165
partnership agreements, 165
part-time employment, 18, 19, 114
passion, 13
pension plans, 129
performance reviews, 125, 155
perfume, 111
persistence, 143
personality
    analyzing, 8–9
    freelance employment and, 166–167
    in interviews, 94–95
    networking and, 80
    self-employment and, 158, 159

shyness, 80, 111
tests, 10–11
personnel departments. See human resources departments
Petras, Kathryn: *Jobs' 00*, 119
phone calls
    interview follow-up, 99
    resumé follow-up, 48
Places Rated Almanac (Savageau, Boyer), 119
plaintext, 42–43
Point of Light Foundation, 80
Pontow, Regina: *Proven Resumés*, 49
practice interviews, 92, 94, 110
pressure, ability to handle, 21
prioritizing skills, 20
problem-solving skills, 97
procrastination, 153
professional associations
    announcing new jobs at, 135
    dues, 130
    e-mailing resumes to, 55
    headhunter lists from, 60
    job ads and, 52, 57
    joining before you graduate, 66
    networking in, 72–73
    as research, 63
    small business, 168
    websites, 54
professional behavior, 87, 143
professional meetings, 72–73
Professional's Job Finder (Lauber), 27
profit sharing, 130
projections, 163
proof of eligibility to work, 145
proofreading, 168
Proven Resumés (Pontow), 49
publications, 49, 81, 105, 121, 139, 155, 169
    Billboard, 57
    Black Engineer, 57
    Business Periodicals Index, 139
    Careers and the DisAbled, 57
    chambers of commerce, 119
    The Chief, 57
    Chronicle of Higher Education, 57
    Chronicle of Philanthropy, 57
    HR Journal, 57
    Journal of the American Medical Association, 57

Monthly Labor Review, 139
National Business Employment
    Weekly, 116
New York Law Journal, 57
professional and trade, 52, 57
Science, 57
U.S. Department of Labor, 119
U.S. Global Trade Outlook, 139
Variety, 57
Women's Wear Daily, 57
Workforce, 57

Q

qualifications
    cold calls and, 78
on resumés, 33
    questions
        asking in interviews, 89
        to ask in informational
            interviews, 75
        illegal, 85, 93

R

radio ads, 66
raises, 126, 127
    asking for, 138
rationals, 11
Ready to Go Resumés (Parker), 49
recordkeeping
    ads and, 64–65
    for interviews, 65
    in a new job, 145
references
    checking, 108–109
    getting permission from, 85
    typed, 85
    updating about job offers,
        134–135
Reilly, Jill M.: *Mentorship: The
    Essential Guide for
    School and Business*, 81
rejection, dealing with, 113
relatives
    employment with, 66
relocating, 118–119
research
    freelance employment and,
        166–167
    on prospective employers, 62–63
    on self-employment, 161
Resnik, Paul: *Everything You Need
    to Know to Start Your*

Own Small Business, 169
respect, 21, 95, 146–147
resumés, 28–49
    career changes and, 48
    chronological, 34, 36–37
    cover letters for, 44–47
    electronic, 42–43, 54–55
    elements of, 30
    employment gaps on, 49, 105
    formatting, 42, 49
    functional, 34, 38–39
    GPA on, 48
    importance of, 30
    lack of experience and, 40–41
    language in, 31, 35
    length of, 48
    organization, 34–35
    posting online, 54–55
    reviewing, 110
    revising, 35
    sections of, 32–33
    tailoring to positions, 34
    writing tips for, 31
retirement plans, 129
Riley-Dikel, Margaret: *The Guide
    to Internet Job Searching*,
    43
risk taking, 8
    freelance employment and,
        166–167
Roehm, Frances: *The Guide to
    Internet Job Searching*, 43

S

salary negotiation. *See*
    income/salary
salary surveys, 126
Savageau, David: *Places Rated
    Almanac*, 119
search engines, 80
self-confidence, 9
self-employment, 156–169
    associations for, 168
    attorneys and, 169
    business plans, 163
    capital and, 158, 161, 168–169
    charging in, 168
    choosing a business for, 161
    consulting, 167
    contracting, 167
    e-lancing, 167
    freelancing, 166–167

personality and, 158, 159
    pros and cons of, 160–161
    researching, 162–163
    skills for, 158
    temp work and, 168
    websites on, 67
self-knowledge, 8–11
    full-time vs. part-time work and,
        18–19
self-respect, 9
seminars, 23
Service Corps of Retired Executives,
    168
skills
    describing in interviews, 90–91
    evaluating current, 16–17
    improving, 16–17, 22–23
    job offers and use of, 125
    maintaining, 22
    on resumés, 32, 38
    returning to labor force and, 26
    self-employment, 158
    valued by employers, 20–21
small business associations, 162
*The Smart Woman's Guide to
    Interviewing and Salary
    Negotiations* (King), 139
Smith, Janet K.: *Entrepreneurial
    Finance*, 169
Smith, Rebecca: *Electronic Resumes
    and Online Networking*,
    43
Smith, Richard L.: *Entrepreneurial
    Finance*, 169
social events
    networking in, 72
solitude, 9
    self-employment and, 162
    self-knowledge and, 8
sports, networking in, 73
Srere, Linda, 76
starting dates, 132
strategic plans, new job, 144
strengths
    in cover letters, 44–45
    determining, 8–9
    in interviews, 96
stress, 112–113
suggestions, making, 147
support systems, 112–113, 116–117
    starting a business and, 164

T

Teaming Up (Edwards, Edwards), 169
teamwork skills, 21
telecommuting, 18, 114
television ads, 66
tell-all strategy, 96
temp work
    employment agencies, 61
    exploring fields through, 27, 61, 121
    gaining experience through, 25, 61
    as a proofreader, 168
    work schedules and, 19
Text Only files, 42
thank-you letters
    after interviews, 98, 100–101
    cold calls and, 78–79
    informational interviews and, 74
    networking and, 71
    sample, 100–101
time off, 128
Toropov, Brandon: *Last Minute Resumés*, 49
Tracy, John A.: *How to Read a Financial Report*, 105
training
    ability to learn and, 17
    inquiring about, 132
    opportunities for, 125

U

unemployment, 57
    explaining in interviews, 92–93
U.S. Department of Labor, 119

V

vacation time, 128, 131
    negotiating for pre-planned, 138
volunteer work
    for career changes, 80
    demonstrating potential to employers with, 152
    gaining experience through, 25
    in professional associations, 72–73
    research through, 63
    on resumés, 33, 40, 49

W

want ads, 52–53
weaknesses
    in interviews, 96
weather preferences, 118
websites, information on
    AARP, 57, 67
    American Management Association, 23
    American Society of Association Executives, 54
    America's Job Bank, 57
    Drake Beam Morin, 105
    Forty Plus Club, 57
    job, 54–55
    by job-seekers, 67
    Myers Briggs Type Indicator, 11
    National Board for Certified Counselors, 117, 121
    online courses, 23
    Operation ABLE, 57
    professional associations, 72
    The Riley Guide, 43
    SCORE, 168
    Second Careers, 57
    University Continuing Education Association, 23
    VESID, 57
    Wall Street Journal, 121
web sites
    aarp.org, 27
    altavistacareers.com, 155
    careerlife.com, 15
    careermag.com, 81, 121, 155, 169
    careerpath.com, 67
    careerperfect.com, 139
    careers.org, 27, 67
    careers.wsj.com, 121
    content.monster.com, 105, 121
    councilexchanges.org, 25, 80
    dbm.com, 167
    entrepreneur.com, 121, 169
    eresumes.com, 43
    fastcompany.com, 167
    forbes.com, 139
    4work.com, 25, 80
    homefair.com, 119
    idealist.org, 25, 80
    insweb.com, 139
    Jobfindersonline.com, 27, 67
    jobhuntersbible.com, 105
    jobsonline.com, 67
    jobstar.org, 49
    latimes.com, 49, 105, 121
    monster.com, 49, 67, 81, 119, 121
    nytimes.com, 169
    recruiterresources.com, 67
    rileyguide.com, 105
    score.org, 121
    seminarfinder.com, 23
    startup.wsj.com, 169
    2h.com, 169
    washingtonpost.com, 49
    wetfeet.com, 169
    workforce.com, 139
    wsj.com, 119
    www.sunfeatures.com, 105
What Color is Your Parachute? 2000 (Bolles), 15, 121
what-if scenarios, 96
women, advancement strategies for, 153
workers' compensation, 128
work habits, 153
workshops, job-counseling, 14
workspace, 124, 133
    disorganization in, 153
    setting up, 144

Y

Yate, Martin: *Knock Em Dead 2000*, 105

THE AUTHOR: UP CLOSE

Janet Garber's career in Human Resources has spanned 20 years in industries as diverse as Education, Healthcare, Banking, Manufacturing, and Wine and Spirits. Currently she is Director of Human Resources at a New York City firm. Many of her insights into the workplace were gleaned from 10 years spent as Employment Manager at a company of 3000, filling 500 positions a year.

As a writer, Janet specializes in career topics and her articles appear in *The Wall Street Journal*, *New York Post* "CareerPlus," and human resources trade journals as well as on-line magazines. She has been a guest lecturer on campuses and at professional conferences.

Barbara J. Morgan Publisher

Barb Chintz Editorial Director,
the *Now What?!*™ series

Cinda Siler Editor

Leonard Vigliarolo Design and Digital Imaging

Della R. Mancuso Production Manager

Marguerite Daniels Editorial Assistant

Picture Credits

Corbis Images 11, 12; **Rubberball Productions** 10, 16, 29, 56, 89, 148;

Artville 1, 7, 17-18, 20, 34, 38, 59, 62-63, 69, 73, 76, 87, 90, 98, 107, 109,

110, 114, 119, 126, 132, 134, 141-143, 146, 150, 153, 158, 161-163, 166, 171-175